DON QUIXOTE

Borgo Press Books Translated by FRANK J. MORLOCK

Anna Karenina: A Play in Five Acts, by Edmond Guiraud, from the Novel by Leo Tolstoy

Anthony: A Play in Five Acts, by Alexandre Dumas, Père

The Children of Captain Grant: A Play in Five Acts, by Jules Verne and Adolphe d'Ennery

Crime and Punishment: A Play in Three Acts, by Frank J. Morlock, from the Novel by Fyodor Dostoyevsky

Don Quixote: A Play in Three Acts, by Victorien Sardou, from the Novel by Miguel de Cervantes Saavedra

Falstaff: A Play in Four Acts, by William Shakespeare, John Dennis, William Kendrick, and Frank J. Morlock

The Idiot: A Play in Three Acts, by Frank J. Morlock, from the Novel by Fyodor Dostoyevsky

Jesus of Nazareth: A Play in Three Acts, by Paul Demasy

Joan of Arc: A Play in Five Acts, by Charles Desnoyer

The Lily of the Valley: A Play in Five Acts, by Théodore Barrière and Arthur de Beauplan, from the Novel by Honoré de Balzac

Michael Strogoff: A Play in Five Acts, by Adolphe d'Ennery and Jules Verne

The Mysteries of Paris: A Play in Five Acts, by Eugène Sue and Prosper Dinaux

Notes from the Underground: A Play in Two Acts, by Frank J. Morlock, from the Novel by Fyodor Dostoyevsky

Peau de Chagrin: A Play in Five Acts, by Louis Judicis, from the Novel by Honoré de Balzac

A Raw Youth: A Play in Five Acts, by Frank J. Morlock, from the Novel by Fyodor Dostoyevsky

Richard Darlington: A Play in Three Acts, by Alexandre Dumas, Père

The San Felice: A Play in Five Acts, by Maurice Drack, from the Novel by Alexander Dumas, Père

Shylock, the Merchant of Venice: A Play in Three Acts, by Alfred de Vigny

The Voyage Through the Impossible: A Play in Three Acts, by Adolphe d'Ennery and Jules Verne

William Shakespeare: A Play in Six Acts, by Ferdinand Dugué

DON QUIXOTE

A Play in Three Acts

by

Victorien Sardou

Translated and Adapted by Frank J. Morlock

Based on the Novel by Miguel de Cervantes Saavedra

The Borgo Press

An Imprint of Wildside Press LLC

MMIX

Copyright © 1993, 2009 by Frank J. Morlock

All rights reserved. No part of this book may be reproduced without the expressed written consent of the author. Professionals are warned that this material, being fully protected under the copyright laws of the United States of America, and all other countries of the Berne and Universal Copyright Convention, is subject to a royalty. All rights, including all forms of performance now existing or later invented, but not limited to professional, amateur, recording, motion picture, recitation, public reading, radio, television broadcasting, DVD, and Role Playing Games, and all rights of translation into foreign languages, are expressly reserved. Particular emphasis is placed on the question of readings, and all uses of these plays by educational institutions, permission for which must be secured in advance from the author's publisher, Wildside Press, 9710 Traville Gateway Dr. #234, Rockville, MD 20850 (phone 301-762-1305). Printed in the United States of America

www.wildsidebooks.com

FIRST WILDSIDE EDITION

CONTENTS

Cast of Characters 7

Act I, Scene 1 9
Act I, Scene 2 48
Act I, Scene 3 67
Act II, Scene 4 77
Act II, Scene 5 108
Act III, Scene 6 132
Act III, Scene 7 153
Act III, Scene 8: The Dream of Don Quixote 158
Act III, Scene 9 171

About the Author 174

DEDICATION

To my friend, Doctor Ernesto Ibarra

CAST OF CHARACTERS

Don Quixote
Sancho Panza
Cardenio
Don Fernando
Basile
Carrasco
Don Antonio
The Corregidor
Gil Ortiz
A Licentiate
Gines
Vincent
Guerrero
Núñez
A Peddler
An Alcade
Toreador
Students
Comedians
Galley Slaves
A Commissar
Maritorne
Chiquita
Dorothea Clenardo
Juanita
Lucinda
Sanchica
Dame Ortiz
Leona
Quitterie
Piquilla

Juana
Comedians

ACT I

Scene 1

The house of Don Quixote. A large dresser occupies most of the center, it is all covered with glasses and faience. At left (stage left), a window on the street. Wall cut short on the same side; entrance door. Stage right, door to the library covered with hangings at the rise of the curtain. Wall cut away, door to the bedroom of Don Quixote. Chests, credenzas, tables, armchairs, etc.

(Basile is mounted on a stool and trying to cover with material the hangings on the door to the library which is walled up. Chiquita is holding a box of nails for him.)

Basile
There. Now, that's good. And in three minutes, Dame Chiquita, I will challenge the most clever person to know this was a door.

Chiquita
Wow! I will no longer have to look at that damned library.

Basile
I'll be finished in three more hammer blows.

Chiquita
Go, go, Mr. Barber. What you are doing will earn you indulgence in heaven.

Basile (hammering)
Which will make me deserve your good graces, Lady Governess, and, also, the recognition of Miss Quitterie, niece of Señor Don

Quixote and I will be the most happy of barbers, as I am at this moment the most adroit of picture hangers. (he hits his finger) Ah!

Chiquita
Take care. Here's my master.

Basile (looking over his shoulder)
No, it's a stranger.

(Basile continues to hammer. Enter Carrasco.)

Carrasco (in the doorway)
Pardon! Is Señor Don Quixote within?

Chiquita (still holding the box of nails for Basile)
Señor Don Quixote? Ah, God knows where he is at this moment. In the moon, perhaps.

Carrasco (coming in)
In the moon?

Chiquita
At least! He left at the hour of siesta with one of his damned books. Once he is reading—

Carrasco (taking off his cloak)
I will wait for him then, with your permission, Dame Chiquita.

Chiquita (turning, surprised)
You know my name?

Carrasco
Is it possible that eight years of absence have made me unrecognizable?

Chiquita
Eh! My God, wait!

Basile
Is it he?

Chiquita
Samson!

Basile
Carrasco!

Carrasco
Well yes, Samson Carrasco, who is returning from the University of Salamanca.

Chiquita (embracing him)
Oh, the dear child.

Basile (shaking his hand)
Excellent friend!

Chiquita
Has he grown!

Carrasco
Eight years of theology and three of canon law.

Basile
And, a bachelor, at least?

Carrasco
Waiting for my degree! But, let's not talk about me, and come to my excellent relative and friend, Señor Don Quixote, to whom I bring the gift of my work, and whom I hope I will find as spry as at my departure.

Chiquita (sighing)
Ah, there—

Basile (scratching his ear)
Ah, there, yes!

Carrasco (quickly)
What is it? Their faces! Has something happened to him?

Chiquita
Ah, nothing! Nothing!

Carrasco
Then, his health?

Basile
Always fresh, and spry.

Carrasco
But, the spirit comports with the body?

Basile
That's where things are decaying.

Carrasco
What! The head! (quickly and uneasily) He could not have lost his reason?

Basile
Lost? Not completely, but there is a loss.

Carrasco
What, this excellent man, generous, charitable, the soul of honor and probity—

Basile (stopping him)
My God! These are always the same virtues—only with armor on the head and plumes as high as that.

Carrasco
I don't understand.

Basile
I'll make you comprehend. The symptoms of this strange malady go back about two years. The lord Don Quixote found himself weakened by pleurisy, which I treated with abundant baths and ordered him to stay in his room. To distract himself, he sent Dame Chiquita to bring him some twenty-odd books, gnawed at by rats, that he had never opened in his life. That's where his misfortune began. God bless him! Romances of chivalry. After Don Quixote had read them, he had nothing more pressing to do than to get more.

Carrasco (surprised)
How could he?

Basile
Look to the side, Sir Bachelor. This door that you see, or rather, that you cannot see, is to the library that we are walling up, Dame Chi-

quita and I. And, it contains no less than 4,762 volumes.

Carrasco
Mercy!

Basile
They are all works which he reads assiduously. From feeding on this nourishment, the imagination of Señor Don Quixote is filled with all he has read—enchantments, quarrels, challenges, gallantries, loves, princesses, giants, and nonsense of all sorts. So, the chimerical creations have become, for him, more than realities, and today, there is nothing more certain for him in all the world.

Carrasco
Mercy on me, so much folly.

Basile
And that is what convinced us to put beyond his reach these cursed books which bring only evil with them.

Carrasco
And what explanation do you plan to give for this sudden disappearance?

Basile
Bah! The first to come to mind! The trouble with him is that, in giving reasons, there is no need to give the most natural ones.

(Noise outside of a voice.)

Carrasco
Is that him?

Chiquita
No, it's that cursed Panza, again! He wants to force his way in, despite me, and he is arguing with the girls in the lower court.

Carrasco
Sancho Panza, the peasant, your neighbor?

Chiquita
Yes! Yes! Another one, that fellow! For the last three days, my lord Don Quixote and he have been consorting in secret, and there is

some trick in it. But, hold on, I am going there, I am. Every time you try to enter, pagan—(she goes out rapidly)

Carrasco
What has she to fear from this good fellow? Please heaven that we had nothing to expect from him! But, I wish to restore my excellent relative to the wisest ideas. Can I count on you?

Basile
Long live God! Señor Bachelor! Razor, lancet, rapier and tongue! All my weapons are at your service! If you have need of my assistance, I am terribly in need of yours.

Carrasco
For?

Basile
The motive is perfectly honorable. You must help me obtain the hand of the one I love, and who is no other than the pretty and adorable Quitterie, niece of Señor Don Quixote, and your relative.

Carrasco
But, you are not noble!

Basile
Bah! As much as she is! The Basiles are old Christians, and I wouldn't swear we aren't descended from that Basil who was Emperor of Constantinople. It was long ago!

Carrasco
That astonishes me!

Basile
And me, too. But a much more serious matter—I have a rival.

Carrasco
Dangerous

Basile
Formidable. The Señor Gamache—the richest man in the county.

Carrasco
Ah!

Basile
Also, Quitterie's father is entirely for Gamache, and very gently invited me never to set foot in his house again.

Carrasco
But, if Quitterie loves you, what do you fear?

Basile
Eh! I fear her! Quitterie, charming Quitterie, soft, tender, pretty Quitterie, but coquettish Quitterie!

(Seen in the doorway is Gamache, dressed magnificently. A valet carries a parasol behind him. Gamache holds a fan, and pays polite compliments to Quitterie.)

Basile
There, what did I tell you? There's that Señor Gamache, who is paying her a million compliments in the doorway.

Quitterie (taking leave of Gamache)
A thousand thanks, cousin.

(Gamache kisses her hand.)

Basile (preparing his razors)
That's that! Hugs and kisses now.

(Gamache disappears.)

(Quitterie enters and sees Carrasco.)

Quitterie
Eh! It's my cousin, Samson. (jumping on his neck)

Carrasco
Are you also jealous of this one, friend Basile?

(Basile, without replying, sharpens his razors together with frenzy.)

Quitterie (turning to look at Basile, laughing)
Jealous? Oh, indeed, if you ever heard him.

Basile

Doesn't one need cold blood to witness what I have seen?

Quitterie
And, what have you seen?

Basile (waving his razor)
Wait, Señorita! Someday you will be the cause—with my own hand.

Quitterie
Fie! Villain.

Basile (closing the razor and putting it in his pocket)
I will do it.

Carrasco
Come, come! You are two children who argue without reason. Dear Child, friend Basile has told me of his hopes. He loves you.

Basile
Alas.

Carrasco
And, you love him.

Quitterie
That's a rumor he's been spreading.

Basile
There, you see!

Carrasco
Silence! (to Quitterie) Señor Gamache is constantly pursuing you with all his gallantries?

Quitterie
More than ever! He's just asked my hand from my father.

Carrasco
Who replied—?

Quitterie
"Yes."

Basile (low)
Ah!

Carrasco
And you yourself said?

Quitterie
"No!"

Basile
Ah, Quitterie! Quitterie, Quit-te-rie!

(Basile runs to her, falls to his knees and covers her hand with kisses.)

(Chiquita enters.)

Chiquita
Alert! Here is Señor Don Quixote.

Quitterie
My uncle—well?

Basile (showing her the wall)
And the library?

Quitterie (struck)
Ah!

Basile (taking his soap and plate)
Quiet! Quiet! Let's have the air of doing nothing. This is the great moment!

Chiquita
Ah, my heart's beating—

Basile
As for you, Sir Bachelor, don't present yourself right away, I beg you.

Carrasco
Very willingly, since I want to observe him before appearing.

(Carrasco goes to a table.)

Basile
That's it, in the corner. You, Señorita, to your flowers! Chiquita, to your housekeeping. And me, to barbering, to barbering.

(Basile goes into Don Quixote's room. Quitterie begins to arrange the flowers and Chiquita to dry the glasses. Don Quixote enters from the left, holding his sword in one hand, and a book of chivalry in the other. He is reading and his behavior indicates through his gestures that the situation is moving. He cuts the last page with his sword, then, brandishing his sword, he comes in. No one budges. He passes by Carrasco and Basile without seeing them. Arrived at the entrance to his library, he tries, still reading, to open the door. Not finding it, he turns the last page. Finally he takes his nose out of his book in frustration and is stupefied at not finding the door.)

Don Quixote
By the beard of El Cid—where is the door?

Chiquita and Basile (turning and playing innocent)
Huh?

Don Quixote
I said: where is the door to my library which used to be here? (he looks around the room)

Quitterie, Chiquita and Basile (acting surprised)
Ah! It's true!

Don Quixote (knocking on the wall)
Isn't there any library any more? I see what it is! It's a trick they've played on me.

Basile, Chiquita, and Quitterie (turning their heads uneasily)
Ah!

(Carrasco indicated by his gestures to wait and see what will happen.)

Don Quixote (continuing to examine the wall)
It's a trick that the enchanter Pantafilando has played me. (Basile, Chiquita and Quitterie breathe, Carrasco is stupefied) My personal

enemy! (threateningly) But, I declare to him, that these jokes are in bad taste, and that's all I have to say! To the good eavesdropper—greetings!

Basile
Good. That's how to talk to people like that! I see there, Señor Don Quixote, someone who is in great haste to pay you his respects.

Don Quixote
Someone?

Carrasco
Me! My very honored relative!

(Carrasco kneels and respectfully kisses Don Quixote's hand.)

Don Quixote (joyously)
Ah, it's Samson!

Carrasco
May God bring you happy days, Señor, to you, who have held the place of a father to me.

Don Quixote
So, you are returned from the University, my boy?

Carrasco
Yes, sir.

Don Quixote (holding his hand affectionately)
Be welcome to my home. I am not rich, my son, the profession of arms doesn't agree with an embarrassment of riches! But, the little I have is for others, as much as myself, and my house is yours! Don't forget it, child. (he raises Carrasco up)

Carrasco
Ah, Señor, you were always the best of men.

Don Quixote (taking the plate from Basile)
There. You are a bachelor, Samson?

Carrasco
Bachelor in Theology, Señor.

Don Quixote
Theology is nice, certainly—but, I'd prefer you to be Knight Errant.

Carrasco (struck)
Your Grace said—?

Don Quixote
Ah! Samson, we need some Knights Errant! If we had, as we once did, some good paladin to uphold right and to redress wrongs, would we see so many girls seduced, so many bad women, so many deceived husbands, so many felons, so many enchanters, magicians and giants?

Carrasco
Giants! Where does your Grace find these giants of which you are speaking?

Don Quixote
Where do I find them? By God! Wherever I find them—on the highways.

Carrasco
Your Grace has seen giants on the highway?

Don Quixote (to Basile)
He asks me if I have seen giants!

Basile
Oh! Ah! But, we have seen more than that, sir Bachelor.

Don Quixote (seated and by Basile)
I have seen more than that!

Carrasco
On the festival grounds, on stage for a penny.

Don Quixote (pushing Basile away and sitting up)
Oh, oh! Does theology trouble this young head? (Basile leans away and points to Carrasco, while slapping himself in the face) He can't believe in enchanters and magicians any more.

Carrasco
Well, no more than giants, dear relative.

Don Quixote (rising)
There are no enchanters?

Carrasco
None

Don Quixote
Then, if you will, explain to me, Mr. Theologian, if there are no enchanters, how is it that it happens all my books, which were right there, have disappeared along with the room and the door?

Carrasco
For God's sake. They disappeared simply because—

(Basile makes a sign of hanging himself and Carrasco stops.)

Don Quixote
Simply because? Let's hear your "simply because."

Basile
Yes, yes, tell him—if you can do it.

Carrasco
Eh! No, I cannot say it.

Don Quixote (triumphantly)
He cannot say it!

Basile (to Carrasco, who makes a scornful gesture)
Beaten!

Don Quixote (triumphant)
And, that's the way, to confound these tortured spirits. Let them be touched by the hand of truth.

Basile
Yes, Lord Don Quixote, but if we spend the day talking this beard will never be done.

(Basile makes Don Quixote sit and begins to shave him.)

Don Quixote (while being shaved by Basile)
And, understand, dear boy, the reason for this persecution is a love

rivalry between this enchanter and myself over the beautiful Dulcinea du Toboso!

Basile
Dulcinea?

Don Quixote (getting excited)
Du Toboso! A beauty for whom I have performed, and will perform, great acts of chivalry—never seen in the world before.

Basile (holding him for fear of cutting him)
Ah! Ah! And where is this Dulcinea du Toboso, Señor Don Quixote?

Don Quixote
No one knows.

Chiquita (grousing)
The fact is that I have never seen her.

Don Quixote
No more have I!

Chiquita
Then, if you've never seen her, how can you know if she is beautiful?

Don Quixote
What does this woman say? And, who dares to doubt that Dulcinea du Toboso is the most beautiful princess there is on earth?

Basile
Oh, God, no one!

Don Quixote (without listening to him)
And as for her chastity! Those who say she had four children with the great khan of the Tartars, well they lie in their teeth!

Basile
Evidently, but watch your neck, Señor Don Quixote.

Don Quixote (more and more excited, stopping Basile often and grasping his arm)
It may be by chance she acquiesced to the solicitations of Don Rodrigo Navárez, Marquis de Mantua, her uncle.

Basile
Ah! You think so?

Don Quixote (without listening to him)
But it was from distraction.

Basile
That's clear.

Don Quixote
And, as for the child that resulted form this forgetfulness—I dare to say he will be the first to admit his birth was a mistake.

Basile (crying)
Yes! But, you are going to make me cut you.

Don Quixote (rising)
I will never shave! I will never shave my beard again. I swear it by the Holy Grail. Not until I have torn from this Rodrigo the admission that he only succeeded in triumphing over Dulcinea du Toboso by appearing in my image.

Basile
Good, but this image will be deplorable if you stay like this, shaved on only one side.

Don Quixote (without listening)
I will remain shaved on only one side. This is the mark that Don Rodrigo will recognize me by.

Basile (aside)
Ah, go walk! Let him go!

Don Quixote
I challenge him, by foot, on horse—by lance and by sword! And I want him to know that nothing will stop me—neither dragons with a hundred heads, nor giants with a hundred arms, nor hordes of Mongolian Tartars. And if he had for guardians Espantifilardo du Bocage

and Brandabarbazan de Beliche—I would wipe them all out! All! (twisting, strangling himself with the shaving cream and coughing) Dragons, genies, all! All! The throat! The flank! Let them come! All! All! A glass of water. I am strangling.

(Don Quixote falls into his armchair. Everyone surrounds him.)

Chiquita
You shouldn't let him put himself in such a state.

Quitterie
Drink, uncle.

Basile (drying him)
Come! Come! Calm down, Señor Don Quixote.

Don Quixote (in a broken voice)
It's good to make him know with whom he's dealing.

(Sanchica enters and runs to Chiquita.)

Sanchica
Doña Chiquita!

Chiquita
Sancho's daughter! Little pest!

Sanchica
Oh! Don't get angry, Doña Chiquita. It's a traveler whose horse is worn out on the way and who asks to stay here while his animal is groomed.

Chiquita
Let him come in.

Sanchica (going to the door)
Come in, sir.

(Basile, Carrasco and Chiquita are still occupied with Don Quixote whose spirits are reviving. Cardenio enters.)

Cardenio (greeting Quitterie)
Many thanks, Señor! I won't importune you for long, and soon my

horse will be ready to carry me again.

Quitterie
The voyager, Sir Cavalier, is always welcome in the home of my uncle. (pointing to Don Quixote)

Cardenio
Ah! Pardon. I didn't see the gentleman. (bows to Don Quixote)

Don Quixote (with a voice from another world)
Is this the knight coming to me on the part of the Archbishop of Turpin?

(Cardenio is surprised.)

Quitterie
Uncle—

Don Quixote (rising)
Tell him clearly, that as of this evening, I will take my lance and go on campaign—and that after three days I will rejoin the great Army—to lead it to victory!

Chiquita
But, sir!

(Don Quixote, leaning on Carrasco, goes to his room, and then returns.)

Don Quixote (to Cardenio)
Don't let them join battle without me.

(Don Quixote, bent in two with coughing, goes into his room with Carrasco.)

Basile (to Cardenio)
Don't be astonished by what you have just heard, Sir Chevalier. The master has certain periods of exaltation!

Cardenio
Yes, indeed, it seems to me—

Basile
Yes! Yes! Oh, yes!

Chiquita
If the Señor would like to freshen up—?

Cardenio
Oh, don't bother with me, I beg you. A chair to sit on is all I need.

(The two women bow to him and go into Don Quixote's apartment. Cardenio follows, talking to Basile who arranges his razor.)

Cardenio
Am I far from Toledo?

Basile
Two hours by horse, but if the animal is injured!

Sanchica
Ah! It's nothing; I took him to Ambrosio.

Basile
This stupid donkey who meddles in my affairs—to make me concerned—

Cardenio
Ah! You are?

Basile
Barber, surgeon, veterinary, to serve your Grace.

Cardenio
Then, I will be very obliged to you, if you would cast a glance over the horse, to which I am much attached. The more so as I must be at Toledo by Angelus.

Basile
You will be, my gentleman. A glance of an eagle eye and it's done.

(to Sanchica) Little beast, go. You who took the horse to someone else.

Sanchica
Shoot! Ambrosio gave me two pennies.

Cardenio
And here's mine, little girl!

Sanchica
Thanks, milord! (aside) I won't tell Papa Sancho, he would take it from me.

(Sanchica vanishes)

Cardenio
Irritating mischance which stops me so near to port! Still, I am not expected till late night and there's still a couple of hours. Let's be patient. (looks outside)

(Don Fernando, dressed for an adventure, pushes the window from outside, not seeing Cardenio.)

Don Fernando
My word—no one in the garden—no one here—I will chance it. (he puts his leg over the window and jumps in)

Cardenio
Someone.

Don Fernando
Cardenio!

Cardenio (surprised)
Don Fernando! You here, milord?

Don Fernando
Yes, yes! But don't call me "milord" here. (he closes the door)

Cardenio
Some gallant adventure.

Don Fernando (gaily)
You have said it.

Cardenio
Again?

Don Fernando
Always!

Cardenio
Just like at the University.

Don Fernando (grasping his hands)
Where my excellent father put you by me as companion and friend. Oh, the happy times, Cardenio, and the friendly madness which began. But, lets leave the past. Since my departure from the University and the death of my venerable father whose soul God has—

Cardenio
I owe to your father's foresight my real place as private secretary to the Marquis de Rio Villegas, Minister of Favors and Pardons.

Don Fernando
Oh! I recognize in that his friendship for you, and I wish to continue it, Cardenio. Money, sword, credit. All that is mine is yours, and you know you can depend on me as long as it is not a question of love.

Cardenio
Why this reserve?

Don Fernando
Ah, because love is love, Cardenio, and when one makes love, I know nothing else but love.

Cardenio
To the point of forgetting honor, loyalty—

Don Fernando
Yes, I'm afraid so.

Cardenio
Oh, milord!

Don Fernando
Don't get angry, friend. It's the profession which demands it. Isn't the most honest bourgeois in the living room often the greatest rogue

in business? Isn't the sweetest guy in town, often is the most ferocious soldier in battle? So with us young fools who profess gallantry. Today he risks his life to protect you from a thief, tomorrow he would be the first to steal your mistress or your wife from you. There are two men in every person, Cardenio. The man who knows his duty and the man who knows his profession.

Cardenio
These are evil principles, milord, and if we were still at the University—

Don Fernando
You would preach me a sermon. Hush!

Cardenio
Eh?

Don Fernando
No! Nothing! I thought I heard—

Cardenio
Your Grace will have the dogs at his heels!

Don Fernando
Ah! Ah! A fine intrigue! Bah! I've got to tell you this—but first, you know that three quarters of this province are mine? Almost to Toledo!

Cardenio
Yes, milord!

Don Fernando
You understand, then, that taking possession of my domains at my father's death, I wanted to inventory my wealth and to see all the pretty girls in the county. To do this, it seemed pleasing to me to do so incognito, and it's in this borrowed costume that I am touring village to village. I give myself out as a soldier returning from Africa. The village girls are seduced by me and the villagers are enraged. At the first sign of the storm, I disappear to put a fire in another furnace.

Cardenio
Strange pleasure.

Don Fernando
Adorable, dear friend. Unfortunately, I ran into some peasants who remembered me this morning and I had to beat a hasty retreat. So, here I am, you see.

Cardenio
And is this what your Grace calls charming adventures?

Don Fernando
Don't you find it delicious?

Cardenio
And do you think, sir, since you absolutely must be in love, that a serious love would be better than all these follies?

Don Fernando
Alas! I thought so once, and even tried your true love—once.

Cardenio
Well?

Don Fernando
Well, it didn't work. In fact, it was in this village. It was a royal conquest. Dorothea had been raised with the noble ladies of Valladolid. Only, I found in her a resistance to which I was not accustomed—and I couldn't penetrate it. I thought by revealing my nobility—but that made it worse. She threatened to inform her father. I saw where it was leading—marriage.

Cardenio
Did the marriage take place?

Don Fernando
Yes—but no one can prove it. There weren't any witnesses—only a priest. But it overcame her resistance.

Cardenio
And Dorothea?

Don Fernando
She made me happy for three months. Then love gave place to logic. Dorothea was pestering me to make our marriage public. So I pretended business required my presence in Toledo and I left—never to

return

Cardenio
And you haven't seen her again?

Don Fernando (seated)
Never, and now I am the slave of another love.

Cardenio
Love! This isn't love. If it were, love would be cursed like the most horrible plague on mankind.

Don Fernando
And in your opinion it is—?

Cardenio
From gallantry and scorn!

Don Fernando
It's all the same.

Cardenio
More than honor and disloyalty!

Don Fernando (jesting)
God be praised, Master Cardenio, you speak as if you know what it is.

Cardenio
And why shouldn't I know it, milord?

Don Fernando (jesting)
Amorous, you! Cardenio! Oh, for heaven's sake.

Cardenio (gravely and simply)
Yes, yes, Milord, amorous, me! Cardenio! Yes, I am in love, with a love which in no way resembles yours, since your Grace takes all and gives nothing, not even his heart in exchange. And I give myself entirely, and I ask nothing in return!

Don Fernando
It's little?

Cardenio
No! Milord, it's not so little. I respect her innocence and virtue, because it is my wealth and I would be infamous and stupid to throw it away for a caprice. I put her honor above my desires.

Don Fernando
Good! Good! Some platonic relationship! It's another way of looking at things. You have found a woman with whom you will be happy, dear friend?

Cardenio
I believe so, milord.

Don Fernando
And the name of this beauty?

Cardenio
There's another difference between us, Monsieur Le Duc. My love prefers secrecy and shadow, while yours openness and scandal.

Don Fernando
Wow! Scandal is a little hard, comrade, and—(rises)

Cardenio
Let's stop there, milord. We will never understand each other. Your Grace won't give up the custom of making fun of what I venerate, and I will be forced to remind him that I respect my lady as well as my King and my God.

Don Fernando (hesitating, then offering his hand)
You are right, Cardenio, and I am wrong. Love to your taste, my friend, and good luck. Of the two methods, the best is the one we like the best.

(Basile enters.)

Basile
By God, Señor Cavalier, I just got there in time. That ass Ambrosio was going to cripple your horse.

Cardenio (quickly)
Well, is he ready?

Basile
Almost, and your Grace can be on his way. But I would advice treating him gently.

Cardenio
Thanks. Here's for your trouble. God guard you and enlighten you, Don Fernando.

Don Fernando
And may He give you a thousand joys.

Cardenio
Thanks.

(Cardenio leaves. Basile goes to the door and watches him leave.)

Don Fernando (aside)
Ah, Cardenio, amorous! Him, too, by God. I would be curious to know her. But first, think of ourselves. (to Basile) Tell me, if you please, do you know someone who could go right away to Ciudad Real for a handsome reward?

Basile
For a handsome reward, they'll go on their head.

Don Fernando
It's a question of a letter to be carried by horse. Only, I see I have lost my notebook.

Basile
Ah! Your Grace makes me think that I have something that belongs to your friend, for Sanchica found a notebook on the road, where his horse fell down. (opening the window and calling) Sir! Oh, he's already far away. But you are his friend. I admit I opened it to see who it belonged to.

Don Fernando
Let me have it.

(Basile gives him the notebook.)

Don Fernando
This is very interesting. Do you know of a horse to be sold here?

Basile
A horse?

Don Fernando
A fast one, if you can.

Basile
I will loan you mine.

Don Fernando
The price?

Basile
The honor of obliging you.

Don Fernando
Pardon, I expect to kill it.

Basile
Then, I suppose, a hundred pistoles.

Don Fernando
Here's double that.

Basile
I am sorry I haven't two to offer you.

Don Fernando
Quickly.

Basile (going out)
In a moment.

Don Fernando (looking at the notebook)
Well, it appears we both love Doña Lucinda, friend Cardenio. She scorns me, and admits you. But you have given me the signal. I told you that you couldn't trust me.

(Don Fernando goes out after Basile. There is a pause, then a commotion.)

Sancho (at the window)
I tell you, I intend to come in.

All
No!

Sancho (comes in through the window)
You see, when I intend to do something, I do it.

(Women come in the door and the window.)

Women
Get out, Sancho!

Sancho (protecting himself)
Ah, sluts. Here is Sancho Panza. (he falls under their blows)

Don Quixote (entering and pulling Sancho free)
By El Cid! What's going on?

Sancho
These pests don't want me to see your Grace.

A Woman
Lord, Miss Chiquita commanded us to take our broom sticks—

Sancho
Well, now that you have them, go stick yourselves, then.

Women
Insolent!

Sancho (jumping up)
Washerwomen.

Don Quixote
Peace, or I am going to pound the first one who moves to a paste.

Sancho
What a misfortune. I had one in my basket.

Women (menacingly)
Huh!

Don Quixote (holding the brooms like a lance)
Silence. Leave.

Women
But—

Don Quixote (ferocious)
Leave!

(The women leave, still menacing with their brooms which they have retrieved.)

Sancho (sighing)
That's the way to talk. But they mix reasoning—

Don Quixote
Let's drop that, friend Sancho, and make sure no one can hear us.

Sancho (shutting the door)
As for that, I defy the devil himself to open it, even if he had a broom and petticoats.

Don Quixote
That's enough! (sitting and looking gravely at him) Have you carefully considered, Sancho, the proposition I made to you three days ago?

Sancho (standing before him)
So well considered, milord, that I have shrunken, as you see.

Don Quixote
And the result of these guilty reflections?

Sancho
It's that I don't say "no."

Don Quixote
Ah!

Sancho
Only, I don't say "yes" either.

Don Quixote
Say something, captious man! And let's leave it!

Sancho
Eh! Softly them, Señor Don Quixote. The fire hasn't reached the church, and the husband isn't with child! If I don't say either "yes" or "no" as yet, it's because I see more clearly than you in this business. As the proverb says: Take the wheat but leave me the hay. If the meal is with the miller, the oats are for the donkey. You never see better out of your right eye than when you've been smacked in the left; and besides, this isn't a sack of chick-peas.

Don Quixote
Good God! Let's leave the left eye and the donkey, and the chick-peas and all the rest—and let's return to chivalry.

Sancho
I only spoke with Theresa, my maid.

Don Quixote
Why this confidence?

Sancho
Good! Doesn't she have to raise her snout because of seeing me bake all night, under the influence of these ideas. Theresa ended by asking me last night: "But what's wrong with you? But what's wrong, my husband, that you toss like that?" I said to her: "Wait wife. This is what it's about. The Lord Don Quixote, our neighbor, has decided to become a wandering knight."

Don Quixote (gravely)
To renew the golden age

Sancho
To renew—yes, that's what I told her. "And since the Knight Errant cannot go without a Squire, the Lord Don Quixote has suggested I act as his. That's the problem."

Don Quixote
To which Theresa replied?

Sancho
Misery! She began wailing. It was pitiful. So, finally, I ended by telling her: "Wife, don't cry. What the devil! The Lord Don Quixote is reasonable after all. He wouldn't ask me to leave my house, my wife, my land before the harvest, and my daughter Sanchica, who's

getting bigger, and my son Sanchicen, and my chickens, my cows, and my pigs who are used to seeing me—all that to run around the world without profit.

Don Quixote
Certainly!

Sancho
"Certainly." The lord Don Quixote knows quite well that the hen doesn't lay where there's only one egg, and as the proverb says—

Don Quixote (irritated)
Yes, yes, but for God sake, let's leave these proverbs!

Sancho
Yes, lord. My wife asked me what your Grace would give me as salary. To which I replied: "Things you can't imagine, nor can I, because the Señor hasn't breathed a word of it yet."

Don Quixote
Very fine, Master Sancho! That means that you do not confide to my care the fixing of your salary.

Sancho
Oh, God. I confide in your Grace like my grandfather. But still, I wouldn't mind having some idea. Let's see, Señor Don Quixote, doesn't a Knight Errant usually give wages to his squire, ordinarily?

Don Quixote (thinking)
Ordinarily.

Sancho
Yes.

Don Quixote
I have always seen knights reward the zeal of their squires by the gift of some provinces which they had become masters of. And I am very decided not to deviate from those customs

Sancho
Some provinces—

Don Quixote
It is even certain, that in the course of the adventures, I will conquer some Great Empire bordered by dependent kingdoms and tributary islands, among which, Master Sancho, you will have your picks.

Sancho
An island! A kingdom! Death of my life, but, as I understand it, if I have a kingdom, I will then be King.

Don Quixote
Necessarily.

Sancho
And Theresa, my wife, will be queen? And my children, princes and princesses?

Don Quixote
Who can doubt it?

Sancho
Me! I can doubt it. It's too wonderful.

Don Quixote
Fine! Fine! It's only because you have never performed chivalry. But you will see much more.

Sancho
I don't say! I don't say! But, why won't your Grace give me, as an advance, some money every month, which I will return when I have my kingdom?

Don Quixote
Look here, Sir Squire! I have told you my conditions. Governor or King of an island at your choosing? See if there is enough for you, for I won't add a penny to you, your wife, your children and your pigs.

Sancho
I don't say no. I don't say no. But, as to that kingdom, where will it be? For if it's in a hot country, as I hear tell of Africa, where everyone burns up—

Don Quixote (interrupting him)
We will make it for you, Master Sancho, equidistant between heaven and earth, between the two poles, with a sun fabricated according to your taste. (rising) By the name of my mother, impudent that you are, I offer you a kingdom and you argue over the latitude.

Sancho
Oh. There, lord, don't get irritated. What I say is so as not to have to listen to a wife who is going to have some "yeses" and some "buts." But after all, long live the chicken! Let her go thirsty. And so long as the island is not too round or pointed, then it's a deal, Señor Don Quixote. I am your squire at this price, and ready to follow you where and when you like.

Don Quixote
Then, we will start this very night.

Sancho
Tonight?

Don Quixote (enthusiastically)
Make sure my things are ready.

(Don Quixote opens the armoire and one can see an old suit of armor hanging there. It is all patched up.)

Sancho (surprised)
Are we taking a kitchen set?

Don Quixote
A kitchen set, ignorant one? Don't you see it's a suit of armor?

Sancho
That?

Don Quixote
Doesn't it have braces and thigh guards, a round buckler, (taking the top off) and a salad strainer, so carefully enchanted by the science of the magician, Tripotin, my sponsor, that it is stronger than iron? Come, we will make an experiment.

(Don Quixote puts the salad strainer on the table and draws his sword.)

Sancho (looking at it)
Take care, Señor Don Quixote, this salad strainer, as you call it, may be put together with string and if you strike too hard—

Don Quixote
Stand back, friend Sancho, and observe the blow.

(Don Quixote smashes the salad strainer into pieces.)

Sancho
Now it's a real salad.

Don Quixote (stupefied at first, then striking his head)
I see what it is! I see what it is! The sword is also enchanted, so that nothing can resist it. On one side, the salad strainer cannot be broken, on the other, the sword cannot be stopped. One of the two must break the other. And the salad strainer was the other.

Sancho (picking up the pieces)
Well, I doubted its looks.

Don Quixote (seeing the barber's bowl with a gesture of admiration)
Happily, the enchanter, Tripotin, seeing my situation, has just sent me, by some spirit, the famous armor of Mambrin which renders the wearer invulnerable.

Sancho (stupefied)
Where's this armor of Mambrin?

Don Quixote
On the table.

Sancho (looking)
On the table?

Don Quixote
Where it sparkles! For it is of the most pure gold! Do you see it?

Sancho
I see a barber's bowl. (brings it)

Don Quixote (smiling)
Ah! Ah! You have, Sancho, a naïveté which I find charming. (taking it) I admit that at first sight this armor does a little resemble what you call it, and this notch made by the sword of some giant completes the illusion.

Sancho
What illusion? Isn't it a barber's bowl?

(Sancho puts it under his chair.)

Don Quixote (smiling at Sancho's ingenuousness)
No, Sancho, my son, it's not a barber's bowl! You will see in your life as a wanderer a thousand objects with the strangest resemblances to ordinary things—all through the magic of enchanters. But all one has to do is put the armor on your head to end all confusion. (gets the barber's bowl and puts it on his head) Have a look!

Sancho
Well, your Grace will speak as you please. It would look better under your chair than on your head. And, helmet though it may be, I will still say that it's been under, rather than on top, more often.

Don Quixote (taking it off)
As to that, it may be! The Holy Grail itself—famous in chivalry—hasn't been used many times, so profanely, that I dare not speak of it?

Sancho
And the hour of departure?

Don Quixote
Midnight.

Sanchica (at the window)
Papa—the soup.

Sancho
Quick! Just now they are calling me to supper! So much to pack up in a hurry. (opening the window) Night's here already. I will take the luggage. I will cross the hedge which separates us. I will saddle the horses. And, on my way to my kingdom—

(Don Quixote has opened the armoire and taken out the "armor.")

Don Quixote (at the window, dropping some of the armor out)
Take care! It's making a lot of noise. (enthusiastically) They are going to make a great noise in the world.

Sancho
Eh! You're losing a copper pot.

Don Quixote
The buckler.

Sanchica (calling impatiently)
But, papa!

Sancho (calling)
Yes! (to Don Quixote) Quick!

Don Quixote
Here's the sword, the lance. That's all!

Sancho
And the armor of Mambrin?

Don Quixote (giving it to him)
Here!

Sancho (disappearing)
Watch out! It's shrew of a governess. Soon!

Don Quixote
Soon! And then, to the country!

(Enter Chiquita, lamp in hand.)

Chiquita
What! Did the traveler leave already?

Quitterie
But it's late. It's night. Samson is going to walk me home. Goodnight, uncle.

(Don Quixote doesn't hear her. His eye is fixed on the beyond. He doesn't speak.)

Carrasco
There he is, in his reveries. Wait! (takes Quitterie's hand)

Quitterie
Always.

Carrasco
Come! It's time to find a remedy!

Chiquita (laying the table)
Won't you wait for supper, Sir Bachelor?

Carrasco
No. Don't wait for me. (in a low voice) I have to consult with Basile. Tonight we will take our posts.

Quitterie
Goodnight, uncle! Goodnight, Chiquita.

Chiquita
Goodnight.

(Don Quixote sits in his chair and gestures the deeds he will perform. He is lost in his dreams.)

Chiquita (putting the plate on the table)
Well, there's a plate! Señor Don Quixote, like the King, doesn't eat off just anything.

(Don Quixote, in his reverie, makes a gesture which Chiquita interprets as agreement that the plate is admirable.)

Chiquita
Doesn't it look nice? And cheese from Burgos! Your Grace will give me news of it!

(Don Quixote, without replying, grabs his serving plate like a shield, and his fork like a lance.)

Chiquita
Yes, yes. Tilt against the food, go ahead. Those kind of tournaments

don't hurt anyone. I am going to prepare your bed.

(Chiquita goes into Don Quixote's room, leaving him alone. The room is lit with a weak light from an oil lamp. Don Quixote, fork in hand and plate as shield, speaks very loud, as if someone were in front of him.)

Don Quixote
And now, we are alone. Know, felonious Saracen, that the time has come to free the sweet Melisandre, and to return this unfortunate princess to her spouse, Gaiferos. (after a silence) You don't reply, miscreant that you are, and you think to shelter yourself from my rages behind the gates of this castle.

(On the word Melisandre, the scene shows in reality what Don Quixote sees in his imagination. The dresser in the background changes into a fortress with its platform, its towers and its windows. Melisandre appears behind a barred window and gestures with her veil. A Saracen guard threatens her and forces her to disappear. A servant woman tries to comfort her; the guard pushes her off, seizes her by the hair and finally throws her off the platform.)

Don Quixote
Oh, cursed dog! Pagan! Thus you treat the faithful servants of your victim. And you have just paralyzed my valor by gluing me to this chair through the strength of your enchantments! But here come avengers you didn't expect.

(Sound of horns in the distance. The Saracens run to group around their master. At the same moment appear knights in full armor. They scale the ramparts, threaten the castle with their arms and begin to demolish it. They are greeted by a discharge of musketry—choked as it is in a vision.)

Don Quixote
Ah, animals. It is worthy of you to employ your arms to fire on these valiant paladins who only fight with lance and sword! Courage, brave knights. Heaven is with you! Come, courageous Gaiferos. Come to the help of your faithful Melisandre! Here are reinforcements.

(Thunder. Gaiferos appears, riding a green dragon. The chateau bristles with monsters which menace the knights.)

Don Quixote (with greater and greater enthusiasm)
To the rescue, knights, to the rescue!

(Battle between the sorcerers and the knights. Gaiferos appears and fights with a Saracen who is overthrown.)

Don Quixote
Victory! All these remain in the pit! Fire the cellar!

(Gaiferos leaves the chateau carrying off Melisandre. The Saracens are defeated. The castle burns and collapses. The knights hold the Saracens in chains. They all disappear. Then it is over. Sancho knocks at the window.)

Don Quixote (enthusiastically)
And, after this, who will dare contest the utility of Knights Errant!

(Don Quixote gets a lamp and is crawling around on the floor.)

Sancho (appearing in the window)
Señor Don Quixote! The horses are saddled and bridled. (entering) What is your Grace looking for?

Don Quixote
I am seeing if some Saracen is not hidden under the table.

Sancho
Are we leaving this fine looking chicken behind us?

Don Quixote (getting up and putting back the lamp)
What would we do with a chicken in the country?

Sancho
Eat it, Señor, eat it! (he takes the chicken, licking his fingers) And the bread! And the wine! And the cheese! (he puts the whole dinner in a sack)

Don Quixote (at the window, ready to leave)
I am afraid, friend Sancho, that you are not very taken with our venture.

Sancho
My word, Señor, it's in the belly you find the daring. Not to take

nourishment is stupid.

Don Quixote (jumping out the window)
No proverbs! En route

CURTAIN

ACT I

Scene 2

A public place in Toledo at sunset. In the background, a street leading to stairs. Large canvas awnings from one roof to another. To the left, the Parador, the hostel of Gil Ortiz. Open doorway surmounting a large balcony encircled by hanging flowers. Bench near the door. At the right, forming an angle to the square is the house of Doña Lucinda. The little entry doorway is approached by a stone porch with three bays which form a terrace. Flowers on the terrace, a small pillar at the corner, a saint with a lantern. Against the pillar is the little table of Juanita, covered with fans and parasols of paper. Against the wall of Gil Ortiz, the table of Piquilla, covered with oranges and fruits and crowned by grand palms. At the rear, children play at knucklebones. Passersby and beggars cross the street with their wallets.

(Juanita and Piquilla are at their shops. Piquilla is surrounded by two women buying fruits and talking to her. All the while she is showing her merchandise.)

Piquilla
Leave me alone about your Núñez—a wooden sword.

Juanita (also surrounded by customers)
And your famous Guerrero, a hand of cotton. The first bull that knows his business and he'll land on the moon.

Piquilla
Yes, yes, at that time, I am sure all the women will bring him home—in triumph! Long live Guerrero!

Juanita
Viva Núñez!

Piquilla (irritated)
Do you hear this daughter of a Moor?

Juanita
And do you see this daughter of Satan?

Piquilla (advancing threatening)
Repeat that!

Juanita (armed with a parasol)
Yes, I will repeat it.

Ortiz (coming out and separating them)
Hey, hey! Nice ladies, put off the party. Don't you know?

Juanita and Piquilla
What?

Ortiz
He is dead.

Juanita and Piquilla
Núñez? Guerrero!

Ortiz
Oh, what a blow! And to think, I didn't see it. I left after the fifteenth bull. At the eighteenth, a beautiful black bull, and just at the point Guerrero put his foot on the bull's head, my bull started up—Guerrero fell—and a blow from the horn sent him rolling underneath the barrier. Ah, what a blow! What a bull! Bravo, bull!

Piquilla
Ah! (she faints)

Juanita
Well, well, Piquilla! Piquilla!

Ortiz
She's sick.

Juanita
A citron—quick.

Dame Ortiz (coming in)
What's wrong?

Ortiz (setting Piquilla on a chair)
A fainting spell.

Dame Ortiz
Ah, poor little one. How pale she is.

Juanita
Here's something to revive her. It's the recent news.

Dame Ortiz
What news?

Ortiz
My God, nothing. We were discussing bulls and all I said was—

Dame Ortiz (striking Piquilla's hands)
Except Núñez was just killed.

Juanita (frightened)
Núñez?

(Piquilla breathes better.)

Ortiz (to is wife)
No! Guerrero.

Dame Ortiz
Not at all. Núñez!

Juanita
Holy Mother.

(Juanita faints into Piquilla's arms. Piquilla is better.)

Ortiz
Now, the other one.

Piquilla (tapping Juanita's hands)
Juanita! Juanita! My dear! I told you that Núñez was invincible! Juanita! Juanita!

Ortiz
Decidedly, I am off.

Dame Ortiz
Where?

Ortiz
To the stadium. I want to know which. This interests me. Núñez, who ordered a supper for the whole cuadrilla. Misery! I won't get my expenses.

(The noise of trumpets, shouts of triumph.)

Dame Ortiz
Don't move. They are coming this way.

Ortiz
Yes! Yes! Here they are! And I am not mistaken. It is Núñez, living.

(Juanita recovers.)

Piquilla (frightened, ready to faint again)
God! And Guerrero?

Ortiz (jumping enthusiastically)
Living as well! Well, Juanita and Piquilla! Viva la cuadrilla!

Piquilla
Long live Guerrero!

Juanita
Viva Núñez!

(Piquilla and Juanita hug each other.)

Ortiz (to servants)
Add fuel to the fire! Here are the toreadors.

All
Long live Núñez! Long live Guerrero!

(Children enter, then men and women playing castanets. Núñez and Guerrero enter with all the cuadrilla, Picadors, Clulos, Banderillos. Merchants try to give water to the toreadors and fight for the privilege. The windows explode with flowers. The toreadors sing a song.)

Juanita (to Núñez)
Oh, querido mío—how handsome you are! And how the women must send you kisses.

Núñez
And I have kept them all for you. (hugs her) Well now, I don't know if you are like me, comrades, but the dust of the arena made me very thirsty and I am waiting for supper.

All
Yes, let's have a drink!

A Valencian (coming between the others)
Serve a cup of orchata, iced in snow.

Guerrero
Orange water! For us? Come then! It's just the refreshment we need. Quick, Ortiz! Some glasses!

All
Some glasses! Some glasses!

Núñez
And here are some legs which ask only to dance. Come children, night is coming; the street is ours! Forward.

(The assistants accompany the dance by clapping their hands.)

Juanita and Piquilla (singing and dancing)
Beautiful, where are you headed?
To love, it's calling me.
And if you said "I love you,"
I would answer "I love you, too."
Yes, there, on my soul, is a girl

Who can pass for sweet and spicy.

(Dancing. The clock of a church sounds the Angelus. All stop and fall to their knees. A moment of rest and prayer, then the ticking of the clock. All rise and the dance begins over again with songs and shouts.)

All
Ah, the muchacha!

Ortiz (in the door of the hostel)
Supper is on the table.

All (agitating their hats and instruments)
Bravo!

(The party rush into The Parador. The passers-by go off. The day wanes.)

Don Antonio (coming out of his house, followed by a valet)
And you say you recognized this Don Fernando?

Valet
Yes, lord, at the hunt. He was disguised and kept trying to meet Doña Lucinda, your sister.

Don Antonio
Watch this door, and if you see him prowling around the house—

Valet
Yes, milord.

(They go off talking. Night comes on little by little. The hostel lights up and, from time to time, songs and shouts are heard from inside. The clock strikes and some women with long veils leave their houses, Bibles in hand, to go to the evening office.)

(Enter Licentiate, followed by a little boy who holds a lit lamp and carries a ladder.)

Licentiate
Will you come on, little boy? It's easy to see you ran with the others after the bulls. Come on, hold that lamp. (the child puts the ladder

against the post and stretches to hold the lamp under the statue of a saint) Eh, fine! Do you wish to take off your cap? Irreverent! There, go down now! (the child goes down and takes off his cap) Come here! No, closer. (he knocks the child's cap to the ground) That will teach you to whom you owe respect! Go, now!

(The child leaves, carrying the ladder. Dorothea, who has appeared in the distance wearing mourning vestments, looks around her as if to demand information from some one. She approaches the hostel and is shocked by the noise of songs and laughter which escape from the interior.)

Dorothea (perceiving the Licentiate and coming forward)
May God be with you, father! (she hands him her offering)

Licentiate
And with you, daughter. Do you need prayers?

Dorothea
Alas! These mourning vestments say that. Pray for a deceased person.

Licentiate
Your husband?

Dorothea
My father.

Licentiate
May he be at peace! And what's your name, child? It seems to me you are not of this parish?

Dorothea
I am not from Toledo, father, but from Ciudad Real, and my name is Dorothea Clenardo.

Licentiate
We will pray for the repose of your father, my child. Goodbye.

Dorothea (stopping him, after a little hesitation)
Could you tell me if you know this city? I am looking for the residence of a certain Duke Ricardo.

Licentiate
Don Fernando?

Dorothea
Don Fernando, yes! That's his name!

Licentiate
God help you, my child. Do you know that damned fellow?

Dorothea (shaking)
Damned fellow?

Licentiate
Ah. Don't ask me where this man lives, a faithless libertine who stops at nothing to satisfy his damnable caprices and his adulterous loves.

Dorothea
What this Don Fernando?

Licentiate
Happily, he no longer lives in this city, where his behavior has caused too much scandal. I know he left several months ago. He's traveling over the land, a voyage of curiosity and pleasure.

Dorothea
Ah, you are certain?

Licentiate
Come, come, my child. Return to your home and never again mention this name, either aloud or in whispers. It will burn your heart as much as your lips.

Dorothea (sadly)
And that's what they all say! One more word, I beg you—but it's not a question of me, this time.

Licentiate (stopping)
Speak my child!

Dorothea (anxiously)
A marriage—is it valid before heaven and before men when it was contracted in secret, in a church by a simple exchange of oaths and

rings at the foot of the altar?

Licentiate
Secretly! My child, this marriage is worthless if God was not represented at this altar by one of his ministers.

Dorothea
But, if Providence, father, had willed that a priest kneeling in the shadows was witness to this solemn act, that he witnessed the exchanged oaths and blessed them from a distance?

Licentiate
Then, the case is quite different, and it will suffice to make the marriage indissoluble—with a simple writing from the priest, attesting the fact under oath.

Dorothea (joyfully)
Ah, I have this writing, father. I have it!

Licentiate
I have a question for you. Daughter, you said—

Dorothea
I lied, pardon me!

Licentiate
Come, I do not ask you your secrets, my child, but if the burden becomes too heavy, you will find a Christian soul to take its part. Goodbye. (goes off)

Dorothea (drawing a paper from her breast)
This paper! This writing. There it is. Oh! I am not your mistress, Don Fernando! I am your wife. The love that I hid, despite your abandonment, I can proclaim it now and make my glory. It is my right. It is my duty! Bless you, divine Providence, who in the ruin of all my hopes saved my honor.

(Some veiled women come with their children to kneel around the pillar. The clock strikes the second call to the office of the evening. The day wanes more. Noise in the hostel.)

Dame Ortiz (leaving her home)
Nine o'clock. The evening office begins. And the padre will scold

me for arriving late.

(Dame Ortiz passes in front of the Madonna and curtsies.)

Praying Woman (without turning, pulling her dress)
You could indeed walk on the earth, instead of right here. Some people who do good by hand, do wrong by foot.

Dame Ortiz
I ask your pardon, Señora. Some pray between their teeth and scorn their mouth.

Praying Woman (rising)
Eh! That's you, Dame Ortiz, who doesn't say it? I thought I was speaking to another. You are truly a good soul, I know it. Let's go together, if you wish!

Dame Ortiz
Willingly. We see each other so rarely. Were you at the bull fights this afternoon?

Praying Woman
No!

Dame Ortiz
Oh! It was charming.

(They go off talking. The other praying women rise little by little, till only Dorothea remains. Lucinda appeared on her balcony during the last dialogue. She bends over the balcony and watches the street.)

Lucinda
No one yet! The sun's already down, and the time has come. Ah, Cardenio, dear Cardenio, are you there? (she bends over farther)

Leona (coming into the balcony behind her, the room is lit up)
Not yet!

Lucinda
Ah! You frightened me, nurse.

Leona
It's only me, bringing a lamp, dear child.

Lucinda
Quiet! (she looks and sees Dorothea) No! It's only a woman praying.

Leona
Besides, he never comes at this hour. You know it very well, dear child.

Lucinda
Do you think so?

(A servant appears in the distance with a light on the end of his pike.)

Leona
I am sure of it.

Lucinda
What time is it?

Leona
Here's a serenader who will answer for you.

First Serenader (singing)
It's nine o'clock. It's beautiful.

Second Serenader (in the distance)
It's nine o'clock. It's beautiful.

Lucinda
Alas, when can we see each other without being forced to hide our pure love like a sin? And because I am noble and rich and he—

Leona
Patience, Señorita. The minister is his friend, and if the Señor obtains what he hopes, we must believe your brother will consent.

Lucinda
Hush! I hear a step!

Leona
No. It's the toreadors enjoying themselves.

Lucinda
It's the step of a man, I tell you.

Leona
Some passer-by.

(Lucinda and Leona take shelter behind the flowers. Don Fernando enters quickly, enveloped in his cloak.

Don Fernando
Now! I am here. Long live audacity! Thanks to the twilight, I have passed Cardenio without his recognizing me. A half hour ahead of him—more than enough time needed to lead to a fine adventure.

Lucinda
He speaks aloud. Can you hear?

Leona
Yes. I think I heard something that sounded like Cardenio.

Lucinda
Listen.

Don Fernando
Here's the Saint! The Door! Now, the servant must come to open it for me. (stopping and jumping back after almost walking over Dorothea who is hugging the foot of the statue) By the devil, what is that? (watches Dorothea, who rises without seeing him, the lamp of the saint showing her face) Dorothea!

(Don Fernando hides quickly behind the pillar. Dorothea, still watching the saint, crosses the square and leaves.

Leona (to Lucinda)
The woman is going. The cavalier is staying.

Lucinda
Peace! Let's listen.

Don Fernando
Here, in mourning! Her father is dead then? Poor girl. What pallor! She is very beautiful. (starts to follow her, then stops) It's the black. Black becomes all women. Charming face! Soul, sweet and tender—and she loves me. Ah, you are a great wretch, friend Fernando. How can you see such a touching creature pass without—Bah! When I listen to my good angel, then what happens will be God's wish.

(Don Fernando leaves to follow Dorothea. Leona hums a tune to alter his intentions.)

Don Fernando (stopping)
Eh!

Lucinda (in a half voice)
Shut up. Suppose it isn't him?

Don Fernando
They're calling me. It's the other one.

Leona
We will see, indeed. But, I bet it's him. (hums)

Don Fernando (hesitating a moment)
Lucinda! Dorothea, oh, the temptation. Bah! The devil is too strong. Goodnight, angel.

(Don Fernando comes forward on tiptoe.)

Don Fernando (with meaning)
It's me!

Leona (to Lucinda)
You see!

Lucinda
Hush! I don't recognize him.

Don Fernando
It's me—Cardenio!

Lucinda (bending over the balcony)
Still—Wait! Leona, go down and—(noise of guitars and voices)

They're coming. Conceal yourself.

Don Fernando
But, I have time—

Lucinda
No, no! They are students who come to sing under my window every night. Let them pass. Later! Quick, hide yourself!

(Lucinda goes in with Leona and draws the curtain.)

Don Fernando
Cursed irritants! How to get rid of them?

(The students enter, armed with swords and guitars.)

First Student
Hurray! Gentlemen, the street is empty. To your guitars.

Second Student
And a serenade to the pearl of Toledo.

First Student
To Doña Lucinda.

All
Long live Doña Lucinda!

Serenaders (with guitars accompanying)
Birds and flowers sleep as
The day flees over the horizon,
But love leads me to your house.
Oh, beauty, chaste angel,
Does your heart slumber?
Let my voice wake it
And let it listen to its friend.

Núñez (at the window)
Hola, students. Can't you go study farther off?

(Laughter of scorn by the students.)

First Student
No, Señor Toreador. It's here that we have some business. (taking up the refrain)

Don Fernando (aside under the arcade)
Ah, the noise irritates you, up there?

Núñez
Gentlemen students—(the students are singing the refrain) Students. (softly) Would you like to dine with us?

First Student
Keep your supper. We have nothing to do with that. We want to sing and we are succeeding.

Don Fernando (appearing)
Yes, but, much louder. The Señorita cannot hear you. Let me.

(takes a guitar from a student and raising his voice begins to sing)

Get up, my goddess.
Then open, very softly,
Your heart to love,
And your door to your lover.
It's the hour of quiet,
Let it open to love.
You can see clearer in the shadow
Than others in full daylight.

Students (meaningfully)
In full daylight!

Núñez (reappearing on the balcony with Guerrero)
Your uproar of guitars begins to burn our ears.

Don Fernando
Stuff them. Then you will see how big they are.

(Laughter by the students.)

Núñez (calling within)
Oh, it's that way. Hola! Guerrero! Ferro! Mateo! All the toreadors! Fuentes! Caldez! Miguel! And all the picadors. To these wise guys

who laugh at us.

(Guerrero jumps from the balcony to the ground, seizes Piquilla's oranges and bombards the students.)

All the Toreadors
Bullfighters, come on!

Students
To the assault! Forward!

Toreadors
Death to the students!

Students
Death to the toreadors!

(The students hit the toreadors with their guitars. The toreadors reply with whatever comes to hand. People come to their windows with lights that illuminate the scene.

Toreadors
Down with the jokers!

Students
Down with rogues!

Toreadors
Get out of here, brats.

Students
Get out of here, toreadors.

All
Bring out the knives. Battle!

(They pull their knives out and pull their mantles around themselves.)

Women
Help! Help!

Ortiz (trying to separate them)
Gentlemen, please. You'll make my shop shut down. Help! (he gets hit on the head with a guitar) Help, my friends!

(Ortiz escapes. The music continues.)

First Student (to Núñez)
God go with you!

Núñez
God with you!

(The battle continues with knives, two by two. Núñez is wounded. The toreadors carry Núñez into the hostel.)

Toreadors
Wounded! Wounded!

Students (cheering the winner)
Viva!

Piquilla (rushing on the student)
Misery! My Núñez! I will blind you, bandit!

Second Student
Archers! Archers!

(In a wink, they are gone. The students pretend to play a serenade and the toreadors, on the steps of the hostel, form groups, eating fruits. An alcade enters.)

Chorus
Night, my boys, is sweet
To dream by the light of the moon.
To see, arm in arm,
Each one with his girl,
How fresh the air is and how sweet.
Admire the shining of the moon.

(The music continues.)

Alcade (to Ortiz, after having looked at them)
Tell me then, Señor Ortiz, who was fighting? It seems to me all is in

order.

Ortiz (annoyed by the calm)
But, just now—I swear that—

Alcade
Fine! Fine! To teach you to play practical jokes with justice, spend the night in prison.

Ortiz
Mercy! And my wife?

Alcade
She can do as she likes, your wife. Come on! En route!

Ortiz
And to say that it's always this way.

(Laughter from all. They lead Ortiz off. The archers push the students and the toreadors before them.)

Chorus
Night, my boys, is sweet
To dream by the light of the moon.
To see, arm in arm,
Each one with his girl,
How fresh the air is and how sweet.
Admire the shining of the moon.

(The square is empty.)

Don Fernando (reappearing)
I was sure that with a little uproar, the police would clear the square for me.

(Don Fernando knocks softly at the door of Lucinda's house. Don Antonio appears in the distance with his valet.)

Leona (opening the door to Don Fernando)
Quick, enter Señor Cardenio!

Don Fernando
Now! (goes in)

Don Antonio (to valet)
Go search for what I told you.

Watchman
It's ten o'clock, and all is well.

(Quick scene change.)

CURTAIN

ACT I

Scene 3

Lucinda's room. In the back, a large window giving on the country. At the left, a small entry door. At the right, the large door of the apartment.

(Lucinda is at the small door.)

Lucinda
He's coming, now. It's him?

(Leona leads Don Fernando in. He has his cape and hat over his eyes and speaks low to disguise his voice.)

Don Fernando (low)
Blow out the light.

Lucinda
Why?

Don Fernando (pointing to the window)
They can see our shadows through this window.

Lucinda (holding his two hands)
Now, you are here!

(Don Fernando takes Lucinda's hands with passion and forgets himself.)

Don Fernando
Dear Lucinda.

Lucinda (pulling her hands away)
What's wrong with you? That voice!

Don Fernando (quickly)
Oh, it's nothing. Emotion, fatigue. (aside) Is this duenna going to stay here?

Lucinda
Ah, Cardenio, you have no idea how uneasy you make me. If you're an hour late, you make me dream of a thousand disasters. I see you all wounded, dead—

Don Fernando (stopping the word on her lips)
Oh! I am very happy. (aside) Will this duenna ever leave?

Lucinda
And apropos of joy, won't you tell me this wonderful news which you mentioned in your letter? The news that can hasten our marriage.

Don Fernando
When we are alone.

Lucinda (surprised)
But, we are alone.

Don Fernando
No, this woman—

Lucinda
Leona? Isn't she always present at our interviews?

Don Fernando
Always?

Lucinda (surprised)
Without doubt. And, as to her discretion, you know it well, my friend.

Don Fernando
Yes? Yes, I know very well, but today, now, I would prefer she were farther away. Very far!

Lucinda
You are my lord and master! (calling) Leona, go as far as the gallery.

Leona
Yes, Señorita.

(Leona leaves by the big door of the apartment. Lucinda sees Don Fernando has softly shut the window.)

Lucinda
What are you doing there?

Don Fernando
Nothing, just assuring myself that no one—

Lucinda (smiling)
This window gives on the garden and on the country! There is nothing to fear.

Don Fernando
It's true.

Lucinda (seated)
We are as you wish. Now, my friend, what have you to tell me?

Don Fernando
Oh. Nothing is so good, sweet, and tender as when I am at your feet.

(Lucinda trembles and withdraws her hand) What's wrong?

Lucinda
Nothing. But this voice to which I am so unused—and this hand!

Don Fernando
If it is more rude than usual, Lucinda, it's that, for you, it has been exposed to the sun for three days, en route.

Lucinda (giving him her hand)
It's true. What were you going to say?

Don Fernando
That I love you.

Lucinda
I know that.

Don Fernando
No, you don't know it sufficiently, Lucinda, for it seems to me that, to this day, I've never said it to you as completely as I feel it.

Lucinda
Oh, how so?

Don Fernando
Ah! Never. I am sure of it. I have never pressed your hand with such intoxication.

Lucinda (surprised)
Really, yes.

Don Fernando (with passion)
Never have these lips been covered with such burning kisses.

Lucinda (uneasy and troubled)
But, no! Never!

Don Fernando
Ah! It's that I've never loved you yet as much as I love you now, Lucinda. It's that I've never seen how beautiful you are. On this road, which seems eternal to me, I ate up the space and my heart jumped in my breast. Drunk with hope, I said to myself: "Yes, she's waiting for me." And, the divine joy that I promise myself, she dreams of it like me!

Lucinda (breaking away from his hands)
My God! Such talk, Cardenio.

Don Fernando
Ah, Lucinda, you are beautiful. I adore you. Don't ask me for more reasons! I don't have any. I will never lose you. I adore you. And I want my happiness without reservation, or I will die of it.

Lucinda (pulling away and running to the left)
Oh! You are not Cardenio!

Don Fernando
Lucinda!

Lucinda (separated from him by the length of the stage)
Leave me! Go away! Who are you?

Don Fernando
Well, no, I am not Cardenio. But I am someone who loves you a hundred times more than he does. (Lucinda makes a gesture) Ah, for your honor, Lucinda, don't cry. Listen to me. You cannot see such love without being moved.

Lucinda
Don't come near, or I'll call.

Don Fernando
Oh, your fright makes you even more beautiful. He doesn't love you, this Cardenio, who in his love lacks the courage to brave your wrath. He doesn't love you as I do. (grabbing her hands)

Lucinda
Ah, wretch. Help!

(The big door opens and reveals Don Antonio, surrounded by friends and relatives, with swords and valets with torches.)

Don Fernando
Curses! Who is that?

Lucinda
My brother! (she faints)

Don Antonio (sword in hand)
Guard all the doors! And if this man takes a step, kill him.

(They guard the door at the left.)

Don Fernando
You won't take Don Fernando so cheaply. (drawing his sword) Who dares?

Don Antonio (lighting Don Fernando's face)
Don Fernando! What did I tell you gentlemen? It's really him.

Don Fernando
Why deny what is evident? Yes, I am Ferdinand, Duke de Ricardo, and moreover, the man who is able to write his signature in your blood.

(The gentlemen make gestures.)

Don Antonio
Stop, gentlemen! Let's first find out what this man will tell us to justify his presence.

Don Fernando
I will say, briefly, that I entered this house because I love your sister Lucinda, who loves me in return.

(More gestures from the gentlemen.)

Don Antonio
You realize, after that, that you'll never leave here alive?

Don Fernando
God knows that better than your or I?

Don Antonio
Don Fernando! Honor is paid only in blood or in honor. How will you pay your debt?

Don Fernando
I will tell you when you have ordered these gentlemen to sheathe their swords and let me leave freely.

Don Antonio
Someone open the door for him.

All
But—

Don Antonio (forcefully)
And your swords in their sheaths. They can be found if necessary.

(They sheathe their swords and exit, leaving the door at the left open. Don Fernando puts his sword in its sheath, then walks to the door.)

Don Fernando
And now, that I am not suspected of acting under threats, Don Antonio, openly and freely, I ask of Your Grace the honor and the joy of calling your sister, Doña Lucinda, my wife. (takes off his hat with a royal flourish)

Don Antonio (removing his hat)
That is my desire, Don Fernando, as it is yours, and within the hour. (to a lackey) See that a chapel is made ready.

Don Fernando (aside)
This problem was foreseen. Come! I didn't come for this, but a great fortune, a fine name, my madness resembles foresight. (looking at Lucinda) And then, what an adorable Duchess.

Don Antonio
Doña Lucinda.

Lucinda (coming to herself)
Where am I?

Don Antonio
Between your brother and your husband.

Lucinda (rising)
My husband?

Don Antonio
Do you prefer him to remain your lover?

Lucinda
Him! But he isn't. It's false. But—this man—I don't know him. I don't want him.

Don Antonio
Come. Don't abase yourself by lying. He's admitted everything.

Lucinda (in desperation)
But, admitted what? But, it is—Oh, my God! On the sacred name of our mother.

Don Antonio
Oh, enough!

Don Quixote, by Victorien Sardou

Lucinda
Let me tell you.

Don Antonio
I don't want to know, except that a man was found tonight in your room, and that this man, for our honor, can only be your husband.

Lucinda
Ah, I am lost then.

Don Antonio
Don Fernando, give your hand to your wife.

Don Fernando
Señora!

(Don Fernando takes Lucinda's hand. She follows him out of the room, protesting. They all follow them. The room is empty. After a moment, Cardenio climbs over the balcony through the window, and enters with caution, calling in a low voice.)

Cardenio
Lucinda! Lucinda! (surprised) No one here waiting for me, and to let me in? I came through the garden. And the room—empty? (looking) Empty, yes? What's happened here? The sight of lights going from one room to another overcame my caution and I risked being seen. But the place is deserted. I must see Lucinda. I must talk to her so she can explain to me.

(Leona comes in through the big door and is frightened at seeing Cardenio.)

Leona
The Lord Cardenio.

Cardenio (without noting her fright)
Leona! Now, yes, I know I am late, you stopped waiting for me, right? But, my horse died under me. I had to come part of the way running on foot. And you see, I came, out of breath, exhausted, but a single look from her will revive me. Where is she, Leona, where is she?

Leona
Oh, Lord Cardenio, retire.

Cardenio
Such language. What's wrong?

Leona
Misfortune has entered this house. From pity, go away.

Cardenio
Misfortune! (the noise of organs is heard) Church music. Lucinda is dead?

Leona
For you, yes.

Cardenio
Speak, will you? Explain, for mercy, speak out and tell me everything.

Leona
Well, it's not her funeral that you hear. It's her marriage.

Cardenio
Marriage?

Leona
With a man who got in here using your name, and who was surprised here in this room.

Cardenio
And she consents! But, it won't be! I will tell. I will admit. Ah, the stupid folly! Open this door.

Leona
Miserable man! They are all there, under arms. They will kill you.

Cardenio
What do I care about their arms? Open, I tell you!

Leona
No.

(Cardenio pulls away and opens the door. He rushes in to the gallery. The song of the organ booms stronger. He recoils.)

Cardenio
Too late! Too late! Yes! (he falls down) Too late. Ah, I am dying.

Leona
Lord, dear Lord. Oh, my God.

(Leona falls to her knees and tries to revive Cardenio. One hears the song of a passerby playing his guitar.)

Passerby (singing)
Goodbye, my charmer,
My sweet love.
My sweet love,
The dawn is born
And the bird is singing.
But be certain
That I will come, my queen,
Tomorrow night.

(In the distance, on the plain, one sees the sun rising. Don Quixote and Sancho on their horses appear in the distance riding through the country.)

CURTAIN

ACT II

Scene 4

A great highway. In the rear, a mill. Brilliant sunshine. Cottages covered with vines burned by the sun. A copse of wood and bushes to the left.

(Basile and Carrasco enter in traveling costumes.)

Carrasco (seated on a stone, downstage)
Don't you see anything, Basile?

Basile (looking toward the country)
Nothing except a white and dusty road and merciless Sun which burns my eyes.

Carrasco
They couldn't have gone far since yesterday evening. But, what road would they have taken?

Basile
I know my Don Quixote well enough to be assured that, a true paladin, he left the care of choosing the road to his horse. The poor beast is used to going twice a week with Chiquita to Toledo to the market. They are in this neighborhood, I am confident.

Carrasco
Let them be. Let's get our breath for a while. This heat oppresses me.

Basile
And, let's drink, for thirst is strangling me.

Carrasco
Tell me, don't you hear something?

Basile
No!

Carrasco
Yes. From that side. (points to the right) It's the noise of a stream.

Basile (rising)
God be praised! We will find some refreshment for lunch and for a siesta.

Carrasco
But, if our men pass by during that time?

Basile
Bah! We will find them again, trust me. Now, Mr. Bachelor, come along, but watch the thorns.

(Basile parts the bushes and enters the thicket to the left.)

Carrasco
I am with you.

(Basile and Carrasco disappear. At the same moment, Don Quixote and Sancho Panza appear in the distance, the first on a horse, the second on a donkey. Don Quixote is armed head to foot. The barber's bowl is on his head and the lance in his hand. Sancho has his hat over his eyes. They are both overwhelmed by the heat, heads hung low. Don Quixote's lance slips from his hand and strikes the earth with a noise which wakes him up and makes him jump.)

Don Quixote
Alert! Here is the enemy.

(Don Quixote draws his sword and starts to deliver a great blow to Sancho who jumps away.)

Sancho (hiding behind his donkey)
Hey, Señor! I am not the enemy. I am Sancho Panza.

Don Quixote
Oh! Oh! It's you! You did well to speak, Sancho. This brilliant Sun has knocked me out and nearly blinded me. I thought I was on the point of a fight with the perfidious Ganelon.

Sancho
Me, I was dreaming we were breaking bread in the shade and were drinking sweet water.

Don Quixote
Nothing prevents us from stopping if you are hungry.

Sancho (red and sweating)
By my beard, what sun! I am tired and the donkey is too. (to his donkey) Poor beast, go. (wiping his face) It's these flies that bother him, but he won't say anything. Go! (embracing the donkey) He's so good.

Don Quixote (after looking around)
This place makes me smile, friend Sancho. For you know that the most glorious adventures of chivalry are always found at a crossroads.

Sancho
It's like the adventures of thieves! Isn't your Grace going to extricate yourself from all this scrap metal?

Don Quixote
A true knight, Sancho, never quits his armor, so as to be always ready for battle.

Sancho
That seems an inconvenient way to walk around.

Don Quixote
It is. But with a little practice—

Sancho
Like my jaw! (removing the two sacks) It has need to work. (taking the bridle from Grison) And Grison, too! Poor chicken! He's hungry. Wait, he's crying. Come on, my dear, here are some thistles, beautiful thistles for the good beast of Sancho! Come, my son, go eat the good thistles.

(Sancho pulls the donkey to the thicket at the right. Rosanante follows. Don Quixote tries to undo the joints of his armor. He gets his right leg to bend a little, but the left leg resists, and the knee grates like a rusty hinge. Sancho returns and watches, astonished.)

Don Quixote
Sancho! Haven't you got some of that oil?

Sancho
I have some lard.

Don Quixote
Rub a little on this knee which doesn't want to function.

Sancho (taking lard from his sack and rubbing)
Yes, but if we rub all this on the armor, with what will we cook supper?

Don Quixote
Patience! This is creaking.

Sancho
Courage.

(Don Quixote bends the knee, which little by little comes out squeaking.)

Don Quixote
That's done! But now, it's the cuirass which doesn't move.

(Don Quixote makes an effort to get it off, but cannot.)

Sancho
Señor, let's try some lard.

Don Quixote
You are right! Besides, a knight must bow only to his lady, and since Dulcinea isn't here—

Sancho (emptying his satchel)
There's the whole table setting, if your Grace will be seated.

(Don Quixote tries to sit down, but cannot. Sancho sits.)

Don Quixote
Ah! Ah! Here's something new. I think, Sancho, that the malice of the enchanter Pantafilando is opposed to my sitting on the grass.

Sancho (stupefied, his slice of bread in his teeth)
Because?

Don Quixote
The left leg threatens to break if I try.

Sancho (with his mouth full)
Devil!

Don Quixote (sitting on one leg)
This my friend, is a great sign. It's a voice of heaven that calls me to be a Knight Errant and won't let me sleep a wink or sit, except on one foot.

Sancho
Happily, his squire can sit with his entire being. And eat with all his teeth. Taste this for me, Señor Don Quixote. You will tell me news of it.

(Sancho passes a knife and a loaf of bread to Don Quixote who eats with great difficulty.)

Sancho
Well, Señor, how are you doing there?

Don Quixote
I eat, Sancho, but painfully, see. (losing his balance and rolling on the ground)

Sancho
I told you to take off your cuirass.

Don Quixote (getting up)
It's nothing. I will content myself with some nuts. Pass me the wineskin please.

(Sancho passes him the wineskin and Don Quixote drinks and passes it back.)

Sancho (after drinking)
There's a meal I'm always certain of. As the proverb says—

Don Quixote (finally able to sit)
Oh, no proverbs!

Sancho
Only, I would like to know—where are we going?

Don Quixote
Nowhere.

Sancho
That's a long way.

Don Quixote
And everywhere! Am I not a Knight Errant? And isn't my duty to protect the weak and wipe out the bad?

(Don Quixote cracks a nut with his elbow.)

Sancho (after drinking again)
Yes, but my realm will never arrive at this rate. And, your Grace ought not to forget that you promised me a realm.

Don Quixote
Rest assured, friend, you are going to have it. And, so as not to change the outcome, get up.

Sancho
Right away.

Don Quixote
Go sound your horn at the entrance to this way. (pointing))

Sancho (taking his horn, which is hanging from his neck)
What am I to do?

Don Quixote
Let the world know that the valorous Don Quixote de la Mancha has left his castle. Are we ready?

Sancho
Yes, lord. (blows his horn)

Don Quixote
Cry very strongly "Toboso." That's the way I have chosen.

Sancho (shouting)
Toboso!

Don Quixote
To the other road now. Sound and shout.

Sancho (going to the other side, blows his horn and shouts)
Toboso!

Don Quixote (shouting)
Tremble, miscreants.

Sancho
Toboso!

(Pigs can be heard "oinking" from Sancho's direction.)

Don Quixote
Don't you hear the guilty squealing in horror already?

Sancho
I hear pigs squealing in the valley.

Don Quixote
That's enough. There's nothing to do now except wait and adventures will rain on us like hail. But whatever happens, Sancho, since you are not a knight, don't let your ardor carry you so far as to participate in the fighting, no matter how great the peril you see me in.

Sancho
Good! Good! I will let you be cut to pieces—don't worry.

Don Quixote
Silence.

Sancho
What?

Don Quixote (breathing deeply, scenting the air)
I scent an adventure from this side.

Sancho
God permit that it be the beginning of my realm.

Don Quixote
Where are you going?

Sancho
Hiding—to obey your Grace.

(Sancho hides behind a tree. Enter a Jewish Peddler with his pack on his back.)

Don Quixote (in a thunderous voice)
Halt!

Peddler (shocked)
God of Israel. The phantom!

Don Quixote (his lance held high)
Here's someone we've been looking for for a long time.

Peddler
Your lordship makes a mistake. I am only a poor peddler going to market in Valencia.

Sancho (from his hiding place)
Lend ear to this, milord, it's a Jew. I can tell by his accent.

Don Quixote
Does he think to fool me by this disguise? You are the enchanter, Pantafilando. And what you carry are the spoils of your victims. Throw down these treasures, vile magician.

Peddler
Lord—all my samples—of spectacles and glasses.

Don Quixote (prodding him with his lance)
Throw down your pack, I tell you.

Peddler (dropping his bag and escaping by the road in the distance)
Help! Help!

Don Quixote (proudly, with a foot on the bag)
There! That's over with.

Sancho (reappearing)
He escaped?

Don Quixote
Like the wind.

Sancho
Your Grace is quite sure we are knights, and not thieves?

Don Quixote
What do you mean, stupid donkey that you are?

Sancho
That the thieves of the road don't do otherwise than your lordship.

Don Quixote (laughing)
Ah! Ah! I have to take it as a joke, friend Sancho, when I see you confound such dissimilar things. Know that what just happened, far from disturbing the peace of the world, on the contrary, reestablished it.

(Don Fernando and Don Antonio, wearing traveling costumes, enter from the right.)

Don Fernando (speaking to an unseen valet)
Leave our horses in the shade.

Don Antonio
Here's someone who's going to greet us?

Sancho (to Don Quixote)
Eh, Señor. Look!

Don Quixote
Silence!

(Don Quixote brandishes his lance and glares terribly at the two men.)

Don Fernando
By heaven, here's a strange sight.

Sancho (to Don Quixote)
Take care, Señor. These have big hats and won't take them off as quickly as the peddler.

Don Quixote
No advice.

Don Fernando
Pardon—chevalier! Can you give us some information about a certain lady this gentleman and I are pursuing?

Don Quixote
I cannot give you any information about this princess until first I know by what right you are pursuing her.

Don Antonio
That's very just. Know this, it is a question of my sister, Doña Lucinda, and that I am Don Antonio de Solis, well known in Toledo. As for this gentleman, he is her husband, having married her last night. Only, after leaving the chapel, Doña Lucinda profited by a moment when she was left alone and fled. And—

Don Fernando
And that's enough, my brother—if it's not too much. Let's go to this mill where we can ask about her without giving so many details and where we won't waste our time.

Don Antonio (pointing to Sancho)
This fellow looks like he wants to say something.

Sancho
If the lady you are looking for is a beautiful blonde dressed in a gray coat—

Don Quixote
One more word, babbling squire, and I will cut off your ears.

Don Fernando (brandishing a gold coin before Sancho's eyes)
Go on, friend, and tell us.

Don Quixote (furious)
If you take that coin, felon that you are, I will nail you to this tree with these two highwaymen en brochette.

Don Fernando (hand on his sword)
Hola!

Don Quixote
I am Don Quixote de la Mancha, defender of tearful princesses. Now I hope, discourteous knight, to end this hour of debate.

(Don Quixote arranges himself for combat. Don Fernando stops, astonished, and looks at Don Antonio, who smiles.)

Don Antonio (low)
Don't you see he's mad?

(Sancho points the direction to follow and takes the gold coin on the sly and pockets it without being seen by his master.)

Don Fernando (to Don Antonio)
Let's go. It's the direction of the convent, as you said.

Don Antonio
I was sure of it. (exits)

Don Quixote
I am waiting for you.

Don Fernando
Yes, yes! Wait for us. (to Sancho) My friend, you ought not to let your master stay out in the sun. (taps his head which Sancho repeats without understanding) And, you ought to shave his head.

Don Antonio (outside)
Brother!

Don Fernando
Coming! Coming!

(Don Fernando exits.)

Don Quixote
What did that fellow say?

Sancho
He said that you should shave your head.

Don Quixote
I am going to shave his—right down to his shoulders.

Sancho
Not today, for he's far away.

Don Quixote
What do you mean he's far away?

Sancho
Oh! They ran down to the valley, hell for leather.

Don Quixote (indignant, yelling after them)
Cowardly poltroons! Cowardly knights! (appeased) But, this will give you some idea of my reputation. At the thought of coming to grips with me—they decamped.

Sancho
And took my realm with them.

Don Quixote
Come along! This afternoon has not been without glory for my arms. Fold up the baggage and let's go tempt fate again.

(One hears the choir of galley slaves that is approaching.)

Sancho (looking, and running back, frightened)
Miserable me! We can die here. Those, we don't want to meet.

Don Quixote
What, then?

Sancho
The archers. The peddler has alerted the justice. Run away quickly, Señor.

Don Quixote (stopping Sancho by his belt)
By death, I forbid you to budge. Trembler that you are, am I not your safeguard?

Sancho (overwhelmed)
Ah, Señor, the archers. Oh, oh, oh! The archers. The archers.

(Sancho hides behind Don Quixote.)

Don Quixote
By El Cid! I foresee here an adventure, beside which others are as nothing.

Commissar (entering with archers and galley slaves)
Halt! Let's rest here before going to the coast.

Don Quixote
Pardon, Señor Commissar. What are these men that you are leading in chains?

Commissar (seated, surprised)
Men that we conduct to the King's galleys. I have nothing more to say, and you, nothing more to know.

Sancho (behind Don Quixote)
Eh, Señor, he's right. This is not our affair, and between the tree and its bark—

Don Quixote
Silence! I believe I'll find some arbitrary act here which will require my intervention.

Commissar
You are saying?

Don Quixote
I desire, Lord Commissar, to question each of these men on the cause of their disgrace.

Commissar
As much as you like. They will be happy to tell you of their prowess.

Sancho
Señor, don't go there. You'll only earn blows.

Don Quixote
Silence, I tell you.

Sancho
Oh boy, oh boy.

Don Quixote (to a young galley slave)
Why are you going to the galleys, my friend?

First Galley Slave (sweet and melancholy)
An error of youth. A box of jewels I borrowed and forgot to return.

Don Quixote
It is permitted to be distracted. And this one?

Second Galley Slave
Too much talent.

Don Quixote
Of what kind?

Second Galley Slave
Pen draftsman. My fantasy played innocently tracing light and fine arabesques on parchment. They saw the signature of the crown treasurer there.

Don Quixote
And who pretended that?

Second Galley Slave
My enemies.

Gines (seated)
Genius always has them.

Don Quixote
And the men who is speaking, why double manacles?

Commissar
Because he's a double rogue who has committed more crimes himself than all of the others. He's the famous Gines de Possomonte.

Gines (striking an attitude)
Say Gines de Parapilla.

All the Galley Slaves
Long live Gines!

Sancho
Ah! Ah! He has his admirers.

Don Quixote
And the cause of your shame, my brother?

Gines
An error.

Sancho
Of youth?

Gines
No, of justice. My only crime is having too much success in gambling—a gift from birth. I can never play without winning. To punish me for this luck, they condemned me to penitence, which is the sea—under the pretext that I have cropped the little coins.

Don Quixote (raising an eyebrow)
That appears quite rigorous to me, Commissar.

Commissar
Oh, well, if you listen to these bandits.
(The galley slaves murmur.)

Gines
Look here—no insults, we are all gentlemen.

All
Yes, yes!

Commissar (rising)
Silence, clowns!

(They shut up.)

Don Quixote
But look here, of all I have just heard, children, it seems clear to me that you are not going to the galleys of your own free will?

Galley Slaves
Oh! No!

Don Quixote
It goes against your natural inclinations. They make you do it through force?

Galley Slaves
Yes!

Don Quixote
And that is what I cannot suffer, having given myself the mission to oppose every bit of abuse! Therefore, our Commissar, who is just, will accede to my prayer to put you at liberty instantly.

Commissar (stupefied)
What are you saying?

(Gines has slid behind the Commissar and stolen the key to the chain which secures them. He shows it to the other galley slaves. They form a circle and are released during the following sequence.)

Don Quixote (raising his voice in a threatening way)
I say you are going to release these men, Commissar, and immediately, if you don't want me to constrain you to do it.

Sancho (frightened)
Mercy on me. Here's something worse than those glasses.

Commissar
Oh, it was to give birth to this novel idea that led you to dally here for the last hour?

Don Quixote
Have you understood me?

Commissar

Come, be on your way man, and return your bowl to the barber without seeking a fifth foot for our cat.

Don Quixote (furious)
It is you who are the cat, the rat, the slave, the traitor and the cad!

(Don Quixote falls on the Commissar unexpectedly and overthrows him.)

Commissar
Help me, archers.

Galley Slaves (free of the chain)
Down with the archers!

(There is a battle. It can be a ballet with songs and dances.)

(The Commissar and the archers are beaten by Don Quixote and the galley slaves and they flee.)

Galley Slaves (shouting and jumping)
Victory!

Sancho
Saint Jacques, now we are captains of thieves!

Galley Slaves (at the knees of Don Quixote)
Ah, our savior, our father.

Don Quixote (breathing hard)
There, my children. Now that you are free by my deed, you are going to put this chain back on your shoulders. (the galley slaves raise their noses and look at each other) In this gear, you will go straight to Toboso and present yourselves to Señorita Dulcinea and tell her what I have done for you. After that you can each go where you please.

(The galley slaves laugh. Gines, behind Don Quixote, laughs louder than the others.)

Don Quixote (raising his nose)
They are laughing?

Gines
Lord Knight, what your Grace asks would be the quickest way for us to be recaptured, assuming we were crazy enough to do it.

Don Quixote
Oh! Oh! And I tell you, child of an evil house, Don Gines De Passamonte or de Parapilla—the rogue—that you are going where I say, alone, with all the chains on your back.

Gines (tranquilly)
That's what surprises me.

Don Quixote
And right away—or I will put you all in chains.

Galley Slaves (laughing)
Oh! Oh!

(Gines puts on a pair of glasses that the galley slaves have taken from the trunk and passed around.)

Gines
I ask again to see this.

Galley Slaves (each with glasses)
And me, too!

Don Quixote
You will see everything right away, bandits, miscreants!

(Don Quixote falls on them.)

Sancho
Lord! (he is hit by a stone) I said it.

(Sancho falls. Don Quixote charges the galley slaves, who greet him with stones and savage cries. Some imitate cats, others roosters. Gines jumps on his shoulders when he's not looking, after which they bring him to the ground all entangled in his armor and run off taking everything with them.)

Galley Slaves
Long live Dulcinea du Toboso!

(The galley slaves escape. A silence.)

Sancho (in a plaintive voice)
Lord Don Quixote—

Don Quixote (also plaintive)
What do you want, friend, Sancho?

Sancho
Are you dead?

Don Quixote
No, but I rather wish I were. Come here, Sancho; I've got a stone in my jaw which bothers me, for I feel an unusual emptiness.

(Sancho goes over to Don Quixote. They are nose to nose.)

Sancho
Let your Grace open his mouth.

Don Quixote (opening his mouth)
In the rear—at the right.

Sancho (hand in Don Quixote's mouth)
How many teeth did you usually have on this side?

Don Quixote
Four, not counting the eye tooth, all clean and whole.

Sancho (frightened)
Did your Grace pay attention to what he was saying?

Don Quixote
I said four, if not five.

Sancho
Well, on the side below, there's only one and a half. And on the upper, all flat and plain, like the palm of my hand.

Don Quixote
Misery, Sancho. That's bad— Peace, I see something behind the branches.

Sancho (falling back down)
Again!

(Dorothea enters, disguised as a young shepherd. She enters with precaution from the road at back and comes forward timidly.)

Dorothea
All those men running through the woods yelling made me scared. Now it seems to me that the way is clear—and—

Don Quixote (still on his knees, in a terrible voice)
Stop!

Dorothea (shocked)
My God!

Don Quixote (flat on his stomach)
And confess, immediately, that there is not a woman in the world more beautiful, more exquisite, than Dulcinea du Toboso. (falls back down)

Dorothea (stupefied, not recognizing him)
But!

Sancho (on his knees, rubbing his kidneys)
For the love of God, young man, confess all that he wishes! We are not in a state to undertake another adventure. (gets up)

Dorothea (recognizing him)
But, this face! I am not mistaken.

Sancho
Oh! By heaven—it is Dorothea Clenardo, our cousin.

Dorothea
Sancho—and the lord Don Quixote, together. Oh, my God, what are you doing here?

Don Quixote (getting up with Sancho's help)
We are covered with glory! And you, dear girl, why are you alone on the great highway, and in this costume?

Dorothea
Alas, it's too long a story to tell you! Suffice to know that, leaving Toledo this morning with a single muleteer, I left him in this forest when he tried to ensnare me in a guilty trap. Happily, I escaped him by flight, and scared by my screams he, himself, ran off in haste, leaving me with his mule and baggage. In this disguise, heaven made me encounter a shepherd who was eager to trade his Sunday clothes for my earrings, with which I expect to get to the nearest hostel more safely than dressed as a woman.

Don Quixote
You are now under my protection, my child. I will escort you where you please—better protected by this lone arm than by all the phalanxes of Macedon.

Sancho (to Dorothea, who looks at him with astonishment)
That's how we are! (rubbing his back) Ouch!

Don Quixote
Go saddle Rosanante, Sancho, and let's leave.

Sancho
Oh! To leave! I am for that.

(Sancho goes into the woods at right.)

Dorothea
I thank you with all my heart, Señor Don Quixote, but won't you tell me from what motive you run around the country with a helmet on your head?

Sancho (from the woods)
Help! To me!

Dorothea
Those shouts!

Sancho (leaping in)
Señor Don Quixote! Señor—ah—

Don Quixote
What's causing this emotion?

Sancho
A dead man!

Don Quixote
A dead man?

Sancho
Yes, in the ditch, in the middle of the briars.

Dorothea
Oh, the unfortunate.

Don Quixote
Let's see. (goes into the ditch)

Dorothea
Perhaps, he's fainted. Hold him softly.

Sancho (shivering)
I saw his boots—oh!

Don Quixote (calling)
Will you come, poltroon?

Sancho (calmly)
True! That one cannot beat us.

(Sancho goes into the bushes. Dorothea looks on, bending over. Music.)

Dorothea
Yes! A young man! Here, here, Señor Don Quixote. Ah!

(Cardenio is brought in by Sancho and Don Quixote who deposit him on the ground.)

Dorothea (hand on Cardenio's heart)
God, how pale he is. But he isn't dead. His heart is beating.

(Don Quixote gestures.)

Sancho
Sir, let a woman do it. It's their job to care for us.

(Cardenio sighs.)

Dorothea
He groaned. Listen.

Cardenio (weakly)
I am thirsty—water.

Sancho
I only have wine.

Dorothea
Give it to me. I am sure he fell from fatigue and exhaustion. Two drops will bring him back to life.

Don Quixote
I know that face.

Cardenio
Where am I?

Dorothea (making him drink)
With friends. Courage. Drink.

Cardenio
I cannot.

Dorothea
Yes, yes! A little strength! There!

Cardenio
Thanks, I'm better.

Dorothea
Don't tire yourself. Lean on me.

Cardenio (astonished)
Oh, it's a woman. I thought so, from your softness.

Don Quixote
Very well! This voice. I recognize him now. It's the envoy of the Archbishop of Turpin who has come to fetch me for the battle. Have they fought without me, young man, and is this the defeat?

Cardenio
Alas, my defeat was of another type! Betrayed by a woman that I adored, and who has married another man, I took the first way that offered itself to me to flee this cursed city which has stolen all my happiness—and last night, lost in the woods, overcome with sadness, fatigue and worry, I fell in this deep gully where I remained for long hours, weighed down by my fall, and where I would have died without regaining consciousness if you hadn't come to my aid.

Dorothea
You aren't injured?

Cardenio
No—unfortunately.

Dorothea
Unfortunately?

Cardenio (with despair)
Oh! Rather to God I had received a mortal wound—and that this hour was my last.

Dorothea
Oh, don't talk like that!

Cardenio
Better to let me die without help than to return me to life and its sorrows.

Don Quixote
By God, child, don't blaspheme against life, for that is to outrage those who gave it to you.

Cardenio
Oh, let them take it back, this fatal present which is only bitterness and despair.

(Cardenio falls and cries with his head in his hands.)

Dorothea (softly)
Each has their own pain, mine is perhaps greater than yours. And yet I do not cry, woman that I am!

Don Quixote
She's right, long live God. This is not the way of a gentleman. Come, my son, no more weakness. Leave the bed and think of a remedy.

Cardenio
There is only one, as I told you! And that is death! (rising) Give me my sword—and goodbye. (Don Quixote looks at him without giving him his sword) Give me back my sword, I tell you.

Don Quixote
It's a question of knowing whether to give it to a sane man or a fool.

Cardenio
Sir!

Don Quixote (without leaving him)
It's necessary, my son, that I hold as insane a man who speaks brashly of disposing of a life which belongs to his country, his relatives, his friends, his King, his God—to all these except to himself.

Cardenio
God and the King are far away. I have no relatives. Of friends, I don't have any anymore. Who can ask me for an accounting of my life?

Don Quixote
All those to whom you owe the example of strength and to whom you are going to give the example of weakness.

Cardenio
And who, without weakness and without defiance, will accept the horrible blow which strikes me?

Don Quixote
He who, instead of searching for his blessing in his feet seeks it in his mind. (he points to heaven, Cardenio watches him surprised, and Don Quixote continues with greater strength) He who doubts, in voluntarily leaving this life, to be greeted in the doorway of the next with the formidable oaths of an irritated judge: "I made you a Christian Knight to sustain my cause, and you fled in the midst of battle. Cursed be you for you are a deserter and a coward." (he points to his sword) And now, here is your sword, my son. Should I give it to

you?

Cardenio (surprised and moved)
Pardon me! I was deceived in seeing you! But I recognize it now. The true wisdom is here. And you are a great sage, from the heart. Give me this steel. I swear to you it will only do its duty, as I will do mine.

Don Quixote (giving him the sword)
About time! But stop, my boy. It's not enough to put a man on his feet. One must come to his assistance.

Cardenio
What can you do for me?

Don Quixote
Two words to some enchanter of my acquaintance can do wonders. Tell me only the name of the one you love.

Cardenio
I can refuse nothing to you. Her name is Lucinda.

Don Quixote
Lucinda!

Cardenio
Do you know her?

Don Quixote
Isn't she the sister of a certain gentleman from Toledo?

Sancho
Don Antonio de Solis?

Cardenio (excitedly)
Himself!

Don Quixote
Well—less than an hour ago, this Don Antonio, with another knight, was searching everywhere for Doña Lucinda, who fled last night to take refuge in a convent.

Cardenio (excitedly)
That of Mercy at Cuenca where she was brought up. Oh! May heaven hear you and what you say be true!

Dorothea
Indeed, you see that it is not necessary to despair.

Cardenio
Yes, yes, but this other knight was?

Don Quixote
The man who says he's Doña Lucinda's husband.

Cardenio
His name?

Don Quixote
They didn't say it in front of me.

Cardenio
He will tell me himself then. Which way did they go?

Sancho
That way! But they had horses, and if you are in a rush, I cannot offer you ours.

Cardenio
I know where to find some. (to Don Quixote) Ah, dear lord, now I thank you for having saved my life. Lucinda is faithful. Lucinda needs protection. Arise my heart and out my sword. I am myself again.

Don Quixote
God help you, my son.

Cardenio (kissing the hand of Dorothea)
Thanks, angel—or woman, it's all the same—Thanks, father—and all—with all my heart.

(Cardenio rushes out.)

Sancho (going to Don Quixote's knees)
Ah, lord, let me embrace your knees.

Don Quixote
What is it?

Sancho
Oh, how well you spoke. And that's the kind of adventure I like. No blows! If there were only a little kingdom, hereabouts.

Don Quixote
Come on, babbler, to our mounts and on with the campaign.

(The flats of the mill begin to turn.)

Sancho
Yes, yes, since we are leaving this place. This way, Señora. (seeing the mill) Ah, the wind is rising.

Dorothea (following him)
Let's hurry! For I am in great haste to get there.

(Dorothea follows Sancho off. As soon as they leave the mill transforms itself into a giant with a scimitar.)

Don Quixote
Oh! Oh! Oh—oh! Our departure won't be so easy, friend Sancho.

Sancho (his face appearing between the branches of a tree)
The archers?

Don Quixote
No!

Sancho (disappearing)
Oh, fine—if it's not the archers—

Don Quixote (looking at the mill)
By Hercules, Here is the most formidable adventure that has afforded itself since our departure. Come see, on the heights, this terrible giant that is preparing to dispute our passage.

Dorothea (surprised, unseen)
A giant!

Sancho (leading in Rosanante)
A giant? Whereabouts?

(Don Quixote is looking at Sancho and Rosanante. While he is not looking at it, the giant becomes only a mill again.)

Don Quixote
The one you see there, who's waving his big arms which are two leagues long.

Sancho (looking at the mill)
That—a giant! Take care, Señor Don Quixote. It's a windmill and what you take for arms, those are sails which make it turn.

Don Quixote (mounting his horse)
It's a giant, I tell you, as gigantic as the most gigantic of giants.

Sancho
And I tell you, it's a mill—as mill-like as the most mill-like of mills.

(As Sancho goes back into the thicket for his donkey, the mill returns to being a giant.)

Don Quixote
By God! It's the famous Brokokuno! And for a long time I've wanted to teach him to live! Yes! Yes! It's vain for you to roll your eyes at me and stick out your tongue. When you lose more arms than the giant Briaree, you will learn who you are talking to. Come on, Rosanante—down with this villain.

(Don Quixote goes out to the left at a little trot toward the giant which returns to being a mill after his departure. Sancho enters, holding the donkey by the bridle. Dorothea follows him.)

Sancho
Here's the lady who will tell you, as I do—Where is he?

Dorothea
Lord Don Quixote?

(Don Quixote appears in the distance, galloping down the road which leads to the mill.)

Sancho
Curses! There he is, charging the mill!

Dorothea
Ah, my God!

(Sancho begins to run, frightened, desperate. He is losing his head.)

Sancho
Señor, Señor Don Quixote!

Dorothea
Take care!

Sancho (yelling)
But, it's a mill! It's a mill. It's a mill.

(Don Quixote is seen in the distance, ready to charge the mill. Two men enter from the side.)

Basile
Those shouts!

Carrasco
Sancho!

Basile (seeing Don Quixote in the distance)
Ah! My God.

Carrasco (running and shaking his hat)
Stop, Señor! Stop!

Dorothea
Stop in the name of heaven!

All (in a loud shout)
Stop!

(Don Quixote thrusts his lance into the mill wing which raises him and his horse and throws them both into the distance.)

All (shouting)
Ah!

Dorothea
He is dead!

Basile and Carrasco
Let's run!

Sancho (desperate)
I told him it was only a mill. (rushes out)

CURTAIN

ACT II

Scene 5

Great hall of a hostel. The entry door is in the rear. At the right, an interior door. At the left, door to the garden. Interior door. In the midst of the stage, to the left, a large niche with a statue of the Virgin. Tables, benches.

(At rise, the muleteers are drinking and singing.)

First Muleteer
Hey—la Maritorne, come here!

Maritorne (outside)
Here I am!

Second Muleteer
Some wine, Maritorne!

Maritorne
Yes, here I am.

Vincent (nosily)
Oh, Maritorne of my heart.

(Maritorne enters, hands full of glasses and plates. She is fat, her hair is ruffled. She is heavily rouged and ugly.)

Maritorne
Here! Here!

(Gines enters, disguised as a muleteer. He grabs Maritorne by the waist.)

Gines (gaily)
Softly, pretty child. Have you nothing to give a poor starved traveler?

Maritorne (simpering)
Yes, some goat cheese and eggs.

Gines
Get some for me, if they are fresh.

Maritorne
I have them here.

Gines
Give them to me.

Maritorne
Raw?

Gines
All the same.

Vincent (going to Maritorne)
Who's he? Always coquetting with strangers.

Maritorne
Peace, Vincent of my soul. I cannot prevent him from finding me pretty.

(Maritorne goes back to serve the others. Vincent eyes Gines with jealousy.)

Vincent (adjusting his rags)
The lord knight must have his eyes on la Maritorne?

Gines
Me? I care for her like this. (cracks an egg)

Vincent (magnificently)
Fine. (goes back)

Gines (rubbing his stomach)
As for the chicken—she's in here. I can hear her cackling in my stomach. Perhaps she's calling the eggs.

Maritorne (returning)
Well? Are they fresh enough for you?

Gines (after looking at her)
Like you!

Maritorne (making a curtsy)
Thanks.

Gines
Think nothing of it.

Maritorne (coquetting and giving him another egg)
Only don't look at me like that! Vincent is jealous like a Saracen!

Gines (stupefied by her manners)
I have to drink to accept that. (drinks) Bottoms up!

Ortiz (outside)
This way, friends, this way.

(Ortiz, Dame Ortiz, Núñez, Piquilla, Juanita, men, women. Then Lucinda enters. Stifled by the heat, the toreadors have their capes on their arms. The women have fans and are using them.)

Ortiz
And long live freshness. Here's some shade.

Maritorne
Ah! It's the owner.

Ortiz
Yes, my children, yes, it's me. Some drink.

All (in strangled voices)
Some drink.

Maritorne
I will run to the cellar.

(Maritorne goes through a trap door.)

Vincent
You are coming from Toledo?

Juanita
On foot!

Dame Ortiz
A pleasure party that my husband arranged, under the pretext that he spent the night between two policemen and he needs to stretch.

Ortiz
And since it's the eve of God's feast, I said to myself, bah! Let's close the shop in Toledo and go see my little posada on the route to Barcelona. We can, at the same time, pick some flowers which we can bring back tomorrow. I asked all my guests to accompany me.

Juanita and Piquilla
And here we are!

Núñez
But—some drink.

All
Drink. Drink.

Maritorne (back with wine)
I'm back.

All (fighting to drink first)
Mine! Me first!

Gines
The villainous world! There's nothing to be made here.

Ortiz (seated)
And you won't wait for us?

(All group together and drink rapidly.)

Maritorne
Ah, but no! Savor it! And that's as nice as I am pretty.

Juanita (laughing)
Oh, she calls this beautiful.

Maritorne (pointing to her chignon)
Only, I haven't been able to put a hand on my pigtail.

Ortiz
It's all the same, you are beautiful all the same! And how goes the inn, my daughter?

Maritorne
Not bad then, we've had a pretty bunch all week.

Piquilla
Who's this?

Maritorne
Well, the muleteers there, the handsome guys. And then, the animal merchants from Pamplona, who passed here with all their animals. Oh, I laughed with them. Ah, but I laughed. Ah, I would have laughed more, if it hadn't been necessary to beat them for the bill.

Juanita
Beat them?

Maritorne
They say that when they have cajoled me a little, they don't have to pay, I do.

(Laughter by the women.)

Ortiz
Oh, oh, I prefer another clientele and places like we are in, I don't conceive that some distinguished tourist—

Maritorne
Well, right. We have here a little lady who is fleeing her home, and who is hiding, for she chooses the most out of the way room, and tells me she's waiting for night to continue on her way.

Ortiz (raising an eyebrow)
And does she pay, this tourist?

Maritorne
Cheerily. Then she had a little lunch, hardly anything at all.

Ortiz
No expense—she's an adventuress. I don't want that in my house.

Piquilla
At least she's pretty?

Maritorne
I have no idea. She hasn't removed her traveler's mask.

Juanita
Young?

Maritorne
Our age.

Juanita and Dame Ortiz
We must see her!

Ortiz
And tell her to go.

Maritorne
Here she is!

Lucinda (masked, leaves her room)
My God, so many people.

Ortiz (brusquely)
Señora, I am the owner of this hostel and I am going to ask you—

Lucinda (embarrassed)
I intend to tell you—

Ortiz
Is the Señora sleeping here this evening?

Lucinda
No, I count on leaving tonight and I was going to beg you to retain a muleteer for me.

Ortiz (grunting)
Oh! Oh! She's not sleeping here. (aloud, without politeness) At least the Señora will sup here?

Lucinda
No.

Ortiz (low to the others)
Neither sleep nor sup. It's nothing at all, this woman. Come, come, her trunks. (aloud brusquely) Señora!

Lucinda
Here, for the muleteer, in advance. I want you to deal with him, for I know nothing about it.

Ortiz (overwhelmed)
Two ducats. (pocketing them, aside) Oh, that's quite different. (aloud) Will your Grace take the trouble to be seated?

Lucinda
No! I only desire solitude and peace. I will go back to my room.

Ortiz (loud, enthusiastic)
The Señora will go to her room! Place for the Señora!

Lucinda (going to her room)
A muleteer! Don't forget!

Ortiz (pointing to Vincent)
Here he is, Señora. Long live the Señora. (to Maritorne) And you say this woman is suspect! Two ducats! Virtue even. (going in behind her)

Gines (ready to leave)
With gold and jewels! Perhaps there is something to be made here. (to Vincent, stopping him) Is it you who will serve as guide for that lady?

Vincent
Yes. Does that anger you?

Gines
On the contrary. Come, refresh yourself with me under the arbor.

(Vincent and Gines go into the garden. At the same instant one hears a great clamor.)

Juanita
And us—to the garden.

Dame Ortiz
Listen.

Piquilla
Those shouts!

Núñez (running to the rear)
It's someone at the door!

Dame Ortiz
An injured person.

(Much consternation.)

Sancho (entering)
No! No! It's nothing—only an armchair.

Ortiz (coming from the room)
What is it?

Sancho
My master, who (gesturing) by a wing of a windmill—

All
Oh!

Sancho
But nothing broken, happily! Courage, Señor Don Quixote, we are coming.

(Don Quixote enters, supported by Maritorne and Vincent. His cuirass is unlaced.)

Don Quixote
Sound your horn, Sancho, and cry Toboso! So that we not enter this castle like some peasants.

Sancho
Good! Good! With regard to a horn, let's try to fix yours.

Ortiz (pointing to an armchair)
Here.

(Basile and Carrasco appear in the rear and listen.)

Don Quixote (seated)
Ouf!

Sancho
There it is!

Maritorne (wheezing)
Is he loaded down! with all this cookware.

Ortiz (coming to Don Quixote)
Funny outfit.

Don Quixote (raising his nose, hand to heaven)
I bless heaven, o noble Marquis de Mantua, (all are stupefied) which made me encounter this disgrace at the door of your castle.

Ortiz
My castle?

Sancho
There! There! Let's leave the castle. Señor Don Quixote, are you injured?

Don Quixote
Injured? No! But broken without a doubt for that bastard Roland has just beat me unmercifully with the trunk of an oak tree. But he will pay me for it or I am not Renaud de Montaubon.

Sancho
Take care, Señor, that this fall has not taken a notch off the machine. You are not Renaud de Montaubon, but Señor Don Quixote, my master. That is to say, the most illustrious knight and the most famished in the world.

Don Quixote (raising his voice)
I am who I am! And I know that I am not just me, but also the twelve peers of France.

Sancho
Mercy on me! There will be a dozen beatings for one man.

(Don Quixote faints.)

Sancho
Oh Señor! Señor!

Ortiz
He fights the country! Wouldn't it be apropos to bleed him?

Sancho
Good! It's only a faint! Let me alone to chafe him.

Maritorne
Yes! Scrub him a little.

(Maritorne pushes back Don Quixote's sleeves.)

Ortiz
Come on! To the flowers, my children, for my temporary altar—

All
To flowers.

(They leave arm in arm, jumping.)

Basile (to Carrasco in the rear, without revealing themselves)
And us! To our disguise! Me as a barbarian princess.

(Basile takes the cow's tail Maritorne had taken.)

Carrasco
And me as an idiot squire.

(Basile and Carrasco disappear. Maritorne chafes Don Quixote with a curry-comb.)

Maritorne
Brother, how'd you say this chevalier was called?

Sancho
It's Señor Don Quixote de la Mancha, sister, with whom I roam over the world to find adventures. And here we found rather more than we were looking for. But, patience—little by little, the bird makes its—

Don Quixote (opening an eye)
By God, Sancho! No proverbs! You break my heart. (looking around him) Señora Dorothea is not here?

Sancho
When she saw that your Grace wasn't badly injured she desired to continue on her way, being in a hurry, as you know.

Don Quixote
She did well, Sancho, for I could not mount a horse for several hours. What we need here is a little balm of Fier à bras.

Sancho and Maritorne
Of Fier à bras?

Don Quixote
A balm whose virtue is such, brother Sancho, that if you ever see me chopped in two in battle, you have only to put the two pieces of me together, right side up, of course—you have only to give me one or two sips and you will see me up and about, more fresh and healthy than a crabapple.

Sancho
By God! May you give me the recipe for this balm.

Don Quixote
It's easy. Let a noble miss take a saucepan—

Maritorne (quickly)
I have it.

Don Quixote
Let her mix a little wine—

Maritorne
It's done.

Don Quixote
Some salt—

Maritorne
There's some in the spice box.

Don Quixote
Some rosemary, and cloves—

Maritorne
Here's some.

Don Quixote
And now, some oil—

Maritorne
Here's oil.

Don Quixote
And let her mix it.

Sancho
Wait! If we improve this with a little clove of garlic!

Maritorne
With a drop of vinegar.

Don Quixote
Vinegar is the emblem of life. Garlic was venerated by the ancients. Go for the garlic and vinegar.

Sancho (emptying the bottles)
With a box of crushed onions and a bit of cheese. Go! Just put it on the fire.

Maritorne
If this isn't enough to bring a corpse to life—

(Maritorne leaves with the copper bowl.)

Don Quixote (speaking low to Sancho)
Now that we are alone, Sancho, I am afraid that these successive disgraces are the result of a great act of stupidity on my part.

Sancho
By God, if your Grace had listened to me when I said it was a mill—

Don Quixote (raising his voice)
You are not listening to me! I mean that I forgot a capital point when I took up my sword and lance to renew the golden age.

Sancho
Which was?

Don Quixote
To arm myself as a knight.

Sancho
Your Grace is not a knight?

Don Quixote
I am in fact, Sancho, but not by right. Since there was no ceremony to put on my spurs and sword and I hadn't received the baptism of some characteristic surname—such as the King of the Ardent Sword or the White Bear or Capricorn.

Sancho
On my oath, call yourself the Knight of Woeful Countenance, you won't find a better.

Don Quixote
That name pleases me, Sancho. It responds to the melancholy of my soul.

Sancho
God help me! Who's coming now?

(Enter Basile as a veiled lady with the cow's tail as a beard and Carrasco as her squire. Basile advances with gestures of admiration which make Sancho quake, then falls at the feet of Don Quixote who looks at him in astonishment.)

Basile
Here he is! It's him! My savior!

Sancho (hiding behind a pillar)
Sir, it's the werewolf or the Enchanted Moor!

Don Quixote
In the name of heaven, get up, Señorita, if I believe your dress— Sir, if I believe your beard—

Basile (tearfully)
A woman, Señor, who will not get up until you have sworn to follow her without argument wherever she may lead you and to avenge her on the traitor who holds her honor and her kingdom hostage.

Sancho
A queen?

Don Quixote (solemnly)
I swear it!

Basile (rising and embracing him)
Ah, Señor, you see in me the unfortunate Princess Micomiconia, legitimate heiress to the throne of Micomiconia in the Micomicon of Ethiopia, situated between the sources of the Nile and the Mountains of the Moon.

Don Quixote
I see it from here, Princess. Continue.

Basile
Widow at the age of sixteen, I had the misfortune to please, with these sorrowful charms, the giant Pantafilando.

Don Quixote
My personal enemy!

Basile
Greeted as he deserved, this vile enchanter, after having conquered my kingdom, sent me off with a great insult, and after this insult I was left with a great beard as you see, which resists all razors!

(She cries in the arms of her squire, who raises his arms to heaven.)

Basile
Oh, lord, come, kill the Enchanter Pantafilando, and with the same blow, separate me from this phenomenal beard which will only fall on the same day your Grace will accept my throne and (with modesty) my heart.

(Throws herself in the arms of the squire and modestly hides her face. The squire caresses the beard in a friendly way.)

Don Quixote (ravished)
Well, my son Sancho, how do you like it? Didn't I tell you so? See now if we will have a kingdom to govern and a queen to marry.

Sancho (radiant, rubbing his hands)
By my beard, or rather, that of Señorita. I think this time my kingdom is getting closer.

Don Quixote
Charming Princess! I am for you, I swear it—but with two reservations. The first is that I will not leave this castle until I have spent the night in the chapel, watching by my arms. And the second, is that this heart, totally full of the inimitable Dulcinea du Toboso cannot answer to your love.

Sancho
Death of my life, Señor! What do I hear? You won't marry this queen? A princess who is perfect, once she shaves.

Don Quixote
Sancho!

Sancho
And all this for whom? For this Dulcinea, who is no matter where—if she is only somewhere.

Don Quixote
Sancho!

Sancho (getting louder, still not hearing him)
He who holds the ring, holds the finger, says the proverb. Take the occasion by the neck—for better a little bird in the hand than a flock which is still flying.

Don Quixote
I forbid you to compare Dulcinea to a crane.

Sancho
And I, I say, that if the mills have left you a little of your brain, you will marry the bearded lady—and that we will send La Dulcinea to all the devils along with her Toboso!

Don Quixote
Now, rascal, is the time you are going to die.

(Don Quixote, armed with a stool, jumps on Sancho.)

Sancho (hiding behind the tables)
Oh, help! Help!

Don Quixote (jumping over some benches)
Let me dismember this rogue who dares lift his voice against the incomparable Dulcinea.

(Sancho crawls under a table and barricades it with stools.)

Sancho
Eh, sir!

Basile (piteously)
Señor! Señor! You swore not to draw your sword without my permission.

Don Quixote (one foot on a bench and the other one on a table)
Give thanks to the oath that saves you, miserable villain, for without it, I would squash you under this table like the cockroach you are.

(Exhausted, Don Quixote falls, seated on the table.)

Sancho
Oh, sir, what I said was for your benefit.

Basile
He speaks the truth, Señor, and my weak attractions don't merit so much discussion. I humiliate myself before the incomparable Dulcinea—and the entirety of my kingdom still belongs to your Grace.

Don Quixote (after tapping on the table)
Sancho! Listen to what this admirable Princess says.

Sancho (crawling out from under the table)
Fine! Fine! But where is this kingdom situated?

Basile
In the center of Africa.

Sancho
Misery! Just what I was afraid of. It's going to be awfully hot there and Theresa will complain—not mentioning the fact that all my subjects will be colored.

Basile
All Negroes!

Sancho
All Negroes! (rising) Never mind, I will sell them!

(Enter Maritorne, carrying the balm of Fier à bras in a large tureen.)

Maritorne
Here's the soup. It stinks like Holy Water.

Don Quixote
It comes just in time—at the moment of beginning this terrible campaign.

(Don Quixote starts to drink.)

Sancho
Let your Grace leave a taste for me. I am still feeling the gallantry of those galley slaves. (rubs his shoulder)

Don Quixote (after drinking)
Excellent brew! Taste, my son!

Sancho (after a taste)
Damn! (pushes it away)

Don Quixote (with satisfaction)
Well?

Sancho (looking at it uneasily)
Hmm! I believe there's a little too much—unless it's the oil. (uttering a great cry) Oh!

All
What?

Sancho
Ah! The door. The door! The door! (escapes)

Basile
Take care, Señor, that nothing happens to you.

Don Quixote (taking the brew again)
That isn't according to the custom of Knight Errantry! This liquor is delicious! (starts to drink but stops and mops his face) Delicious—that keeps you active—makes you shiver—this oil is hot. Where is the door?

Basile
Over there.

Don Quixote (staggering towards the door)
That way, good.

Basile
No, this way.

Don Quixote (ghastly, not seeing, but always dignified)
Ah, this way. (going) Too much oil! Fier à bras ought not to have so much oil.

(Don Quixote exits at rear. Basile breaks into laughter and removes his beard.)

Basile
The farce is playing and we have him.

Carrasco
All we have to do is get him to take the road to the village tomorrow. Once home we shall see to things as we like.

Basile
Provided some whim doesn't make him leave tonight.

Carrasco
Which is what we must still be careful about.

Basile
Hush! Here's our Innkeeper and all his company. Let's not lose sight of our knight.

(Basile and Carrasco exit. Ortiz and his group return with flowers.)

Juanita
There's my harvest!

Piquilla
And mine!

All
And ours.

Ortiz
That's what makes Toledo an altar that outshines the others. Night is coming—we must be on our way. Close the courtyard doors, children.

(They spread the flowers on the table. People go in and out with lanterns.)

Dame Ortiz
And, this lady who wants to leave at nightfall?

Ortiz
Ah, I forgot. (knocking on Lucinda's door) Señora, it's night time.

Lucinda
Your man is ready?

Ortiz
Always! Vincent, the house muleteer. Well, where is he?

Maritorne
Vincent!

All
Vincent.

Gines (in a corner)
Don't bother calling. He's in the stable, dead drunk.

Ortiz (shocked)
Ah!

Gines
But I can replace him.

Ortiz
You, friend! But we don't know you.

Gines
Here are my papers. Certificate from the commissioner, passes from the mayor.

Ortiz (examining)
But, yes—precisely. Very much in order.

Gines (aside)
I really think all the commissioner's seals are useful.

Ortiz
Señora, here's a man to whom you can—(knocking on the hostel door)

Lucinda
That voice!

Ortiz
Travelers! Open.

Maritorne
Some cavaliers.

Lucinda (terrified)
Ah, my God! I am lost.

All
Lost!

Lucinda
Oh! From pity, save me! Hide me! Don't let them find me. Save me.

(Lucinda's mask falls off.)

Juanita
Doña Lucinda!

Lucinda
You know me?

Juanita
I think our shop is by your door, Señora. But rest easy, Señora. They won't carry you off. (to Núñez) Come on, alert my boys.

Núñez and the Toreadors (drawing their knives)
They are ready!

Lucinda (horrified)
Arms? Against my brother?

Juanita
Your brother?

Don Antonio (outside)
Over this way, Fernando.

Lucinda (overwhelmed)
There he is. Oh, Madonna! Save me!

(Lucinda falls to her knees at the foot of a pillar.)

Juanita
No knives, you fellows! But a trick. That's a woman's business.

Núñez
But—

Juanita
Shut up! (to Lucinda) Don't budge. I will save you.

(Juanita throws all the flowers on Lucinda. Others join her in covering Lucinda and Lucinda disappears under the flowers.)

Juanita
Watch out for tattle tales.

(Don Fernando comes in from the rear with men armed with torches.)

Don Fernando
Hola, Innkeeper. Haven't you some lady making a trip hereabouts?

Ortiz
Oh, several ladies who are helping me make an altar for the Feast Day.

Don Antonio
And, in these rooms?

Ortiz
Nobody!

Don Fernando
We had been given good information about you.

Ortiz
If your Grace cares to see?

Don Fernando
Yes, I wish to see.

(Don Fernando goes into the room at right, followed by Don Antonio. Juanita begins to sing while stringing the garlands.)

Juanita (singing)
Daughter, listen to me.
You're going to marry the King.
Daddy, I'm going to marry
The one I love.
Soldiers, soldiers,
Arrest her.
But the girl is gone.
The soldiers look everywhere
But cannot find her.

(Meanwhile Don Antonio and Don Fernando search, but find no

one.)

Juanita
They looked here.
They looked there.
But they couldn't find her
Anywhere.

(to Don Fernando) Will your Grace throw some flowers to the Madonna?

Don Fernando
Here's for you. (gives her a gold coin) And, (throwing flowers) here's for her.

Juanita (curtseying)
Thanks for her and for me.

Don Antonio
Nothing!

Don Fernando (loud)
Let's be on our way.

(Exit Don Fernando and Don Antonio.)

Juanita
Lights for the gentlemen, so they can see more clearly.

(Maritorne and the valet follow Don Fernando and Don Antonio. Lucinda starts to come out of the flowers.)

Juanita
Not yet.

(Juanita listens. The sound of Don Antonio and Don Fernando leaving can be heard.)

All
They're gone!

(Juanita pulls Lucinda from the midst of the flowers.)

Juanita
Saved!

All (singing)
They looked here.
They looked there.
They couldn't find her
Anywhere.

CURTAIN

ACT II

Scene 6

The courtyard of the hostel, dimly lit by the moon which cannot yet be seen. To the left, the house. A little window on the side. Entry door. To the right, a stable, hay, etc. In the rear, a large wall with a door. Beyond that, the country. A well to the right with jugs and jars.

At rise, Don Quixote is leaning on the well, head in his hands. Sancho is stretched on the hay. Both are profoundly overwhelmed.

Don Quixote (in a miserable voice)
Sancho!

Sancho (sighing)
Ah!

Don Quixote
Don't tremble, brother. It's nothing.

Sancho (sighing)
Ah.

Don Quixote
What would you say if you had to cross the ocean to conquer the Golden Fleece? Here it's only the balm of Fier à bras.

Sancho (furiously rising and punching the haystack)
Croak! Croak! Croak! The son of a carrion that invented it.

Don Quixote
A little water will help us, my son? But this is the point I told you of. (plunging his head into a bucket) It's as if I weren't an armed knight. Everything is going against us. The noble lord of the castle could not refuse me such a favor.

Sancho (trying to sleep)
Death of my life. I have the hunger of a rabid person.

Don Quixote
You are hungry?

Sancho
The balm has cracked my stomach. It's empty.

Don Quixote
Sleep then. He who sleeps, sups.

Sancho
Yes, but he who sups sleeps even better. The smell of hay gives me an appetite.

(Sancho stretched out. Don Quixote is pacing up and down. Silence.)

Don Quixote
Sancho, did you notice the tender and languorous look that the lovely Princess who accompanies the Marquis cast on me?

Sancho
Who, the serving girl who watered me so well?

Don Quixote
Herself. If I correctly understood her last look, it was a formal invitation to force the door of her chamber.

Sancho (in a bad temper)
Your Grace gives me a pain. It's the dishwasher of this cursed barracks? And ugly as three little pigs!

Don Quixote
Always enchantments pursue you, Sancho, and make you mistake a giant for a windmill.

Sancho
Wait, Señor, I am not in a good mood. Leave me to sleep, or otherwise I will tell you some things—some things that—(falls asleep)

Don Quixote
Still, unfortunate Princess, all your advances are wasted. This heart is filled by a single image. O Dulcinea, Dulcinea!

(Don Quixote marches up and down with his lance on his shoulder.)

Don Quixote
Let's begin the vigil.

(A moment of silence. Don Quixote leaves by the door at the rear. At the same moment, Vincent enters from the right. He is drunk.)

Vincent
I believe that rogue of a Gines made me drink more than I could hold. Here! The cellar. (looking in the well) No, it's a dormer window. I am going to find Maritorne. (goes to house and calls) Maritorne. Mari-tone. (throws a stone at the window) Maritorne. (tenderly) It's me, your little Vincent. (furious, throws a big stone) But devil's sister, do you intend to open for me?

(Maritorne appears at the little window, candle in hand. She is in undress.)

Maritorne
It's you, you drunk.

Vincent
It's me, pretty.

Maritorne
I ought to let you sleep in the stable with your look-alikes.

Vincent
My dear heart, I assure you I am sober.

Maritorne
Fine. I am going to see about that.

(Maritorne closes the window and disappears.)

Don Quixote (startled by the noise)
Hey!

Vincent (humming)
Maritorne's a bitch.
A big bitch.
A blind bitch.

Don Quixote (listening)
A serenade!

Maritorne (coming out and looking for Vincent)
Monstrous man! To say you love like this—go on, where are you? I have put out the candle. If the boss suspects, he'll kick us both out. Where are you, renegade?

(Groping around, Maritorne ends up near Don Quixote who takes her in his arms.)

Don Quixote
I wish I might show myself more worthy, high and charming lady, of the infinite favor your are doing me.

Maritorne (shocked)
Hey, who? What?

Don Quixote (drawing her tenderly to his heart)
But I have sworn fidelity to the incomparable Dulcinea.

Maritorne
It's the madman! Do you want me to beat you?

Don Quixote
No, no, don't insist. For in spite of the attraction that I feel—

Vincent (returning)
Ah, gypsy!

Don Quixote
Hey—

Vincent
Oh, you know how to grope for another.

(Vincent falls on Don Quixote with his fists. Don Quixote slips and falls while struggling with him.)

Maritorne
Help! Help me!

(Maritorne pulls away and falls over Sancho who awakens with a start.)

Sancho
Thieves!

(Sancho beats Maritorne who returns his blows.)

Don Quixote
Ah, traitor, cowardly magician.

Sancho
This little bitch again?

Maritorne
Murderer! Murderer!

(They end, all four, by rolling on the ground. Maritorne gets loose and runs off, then Vincent, leaving only Don Quixote and Sancho. Sancho continues to fight, now it is only Don Quixote that he is hitting.)

Sancho
I've got you, sorcerer.

Don Quixote
You will die, magician!

Sancho (recognizing him)
My master!

Don Quixote
Sancho!

Sancho
Well here's proof there's magic in our affair. I overthrew a horrible ghoul and it's on your lordship that I—

Don Quixote
A ghoul?

Sancho
Still, I've got a fist full of his hair.

Don Quixote
I will tell you, Sancho that this reappearance of magic ought not to astonish you. It's sure that the vigil over arms is concentrating all the efforts of our infernal enemies against us, to disgust us with divine chivalry.

Sancho
Ah, well! That's done it for me—bad meal and bad sleep. (finding his hole in the hay) God, how hungry I am! (he disappears in the hay, except for his head) The odor of hay still gives me an appetite. (Sancho falls asleep. The clouds which cover the sky begin to separate, lit by the moon.)

Don Quixote (rising)
It's a question of holding on, friend, for this hostel has the effect on me of a nest of sorcerers—but I defy them. They and all their demonic sequels. Appear marauders, felonious knights, perfidious chatelains. The one who defies you is the intrepid Don Quixote—Knight of the Woeful Countenance.

(The clouds dissipate and images of knights, princesses, giants and towers appear, then bit by bit evaporate, leaving an empty sky.)

Don Quixote
Who has seen my victory over these infernal legions? Window of heaven, mirrors of earth, eye of paradise. Doubtless the one I love looks at you as I do at this moment, and you are witness to my sadness as well as her regrets.

(The face of Dulcinea, looking sad, forms on the face of the moon.)

Don Quixote
There she is! I read her chagrin on her face. (Dulcinea's eyebrows contract and she seems to weep) You weep, weep, O lady, you weep over my departure. Dry your tears and instead smile at the thought that it is for you that I cover myself with glory. (Dulcinea seems to

smile) And that, before long, I will place at your feet a thousand laurels and as many crowns. (he kneels, the moon laughs)

Don Quixote
O joy, she laughs, she laughs uproariously.

(Slowly the moon disappears behind new clouds that are forming.)

Sancho (turning in the hay and dreaming)
Theresa, my wife! Theresa, oh Theresa! But answer me, will you? (he kicks and wakes up) Ouf! It was a nightmare. It's hunger. I have a hunger cramp. Is there nothing to put between my teeth? (gets up and goes to the jugs leaning against the wall) Watch out! Some jugs. Some crusts in reserve for the chickens. (plunges his hand into a jar) Nothing! (then into another) Yes—some dry figs! A fistful, I am saved. (unable to pull his hand out of the jar) This is—hey, hey. (still cannot release his hand) Miserable me! My fist is stuck there. Sorcery. Bitch of a jug! Just wait. (seeing Don Quixote on his knees) An idiot! This is my affair.

(Sancho breaks the jug over Don Quixote's helmet. The jug falls in pieces. Don Quixote jumps up.)

Don Quixote
To arms!

Sancho (stupefied)
My master—

Don Quixote (stabbing out right and left)
Avant Turpin! Here's Ganelon attacking our two wings at the same time! Courage, knights! To the rescue! Toboso! Toboso!

(Don Quixote beats the jugs, the wall and the well. He strikes the edge of the well and Sancho, losing his balance falls into the well opening.)

Sancho
Eh! Help! Help! I am falling.

Don Quixote (pushing him into the well)
To the moat, miscreants, to the moat.

(Enter Ortiz and his group.)

Ortiz (furious, his halberd in his hand)
But, by the devil's horns, what is going on?

All
What a racket!

Ortiz
He's strangling someone.

All (stopping Don Quixote)
Stop! It's Sancho!

Don Quixote
It's Sancho?

Sancho
Yes, it's me! Me! Me!

(Sancho gets back to his feet.)

Ortiz
And it's for this pretty work that he puts the whole hostel up in the air!

Basile
Patience, Innkeeper. Day is here.

Ortiz (exasperated, low to Basile without Don Quixote hearing him)
I have had enough of your madman. He'll run everybody out of my house. Let him decamp.

(Don Quixote falls on his knees behind Ortiz when he wasn't watching.)

Don Quixote
Señor chatelain—

Ortiz
Huh?

Don Quixote
Now that I have gloriously completed the vigil of arms, I won't rise until you have crowned me as a knight.

Ortiz
Oh, right away. (to Basile) Since he's leaving.

Don Quixote (ravished)
Ah, lord—

Ortiz
Yes, yes, we are going to satisfy you. (to Maritorne) Pass me my cookbook. Piquilla, Juanita! The frying pan.

(Ortiz throws them his apron which they put over the head of Don Quixote, each holding a lamp.)

Ortiz (to Núñez and the valet)
Here are the witnesses. And you, (to Sancho) the candle.

Basile
Here's the sword, Señor.

Carrasco
And the spurs!

Ortiz (opening the book and speaking rapidly)
Let's begin! (muttering) To make a dish of rabbit, cut it in pieces, cover it with bouillon, cook until well done. Season it, then put in some wine, and take a pinch of farina—with an onion, and add a little vinegar, spices and cloves of garlic, etc. (striking Don Quixote's shoulder with the flat of his sword) And serve, serve, serve hot. (giving Don Quixote the sword) There, it's done. And now, open the door so he can leave.

(Maritorne goes to open the door in the rear. Day starts to come on.)

Don Quixote (on his knees)
O noble ladies, what are your names?

Piquilla
Piquilla!

Juanita
And Juanita!

Don Quixote
For love of me, young ladies, henceforth, call yourselves Doña Piquilla and Doña Juanita.

Juanita and Piquilla (curtsying)
We won't fail to do so.

(They release the apron which falls over his nose and covers the broken bowl.)

Ortiz
Let's go, on your way, on your way, chevalier.

Basile
And remember, lord, that you are escorting me.

Don Quixote
Yes, Princess, but before following you to the ends of the earth, I should settle accounts with this vile magician who pestered me all night and who is assuredly hidden in this house.

(Don Quixote goes to enter the hostel.)

Maritorne (seeing Basile)
Oh, my cow's tail.

(She tears the beard from Basile.)

Sancho
Basile!

Carrasco and Basile
Ah!

Don Quixote (stupefied)
Oh, oh, what does this mean? And how can you explain to me how the Barber Basile and the Princess Micomicona are really the same person.

Basile
It's the magic that—

Don Quixote (raising his eyebrows)
That is enough, Señor, wearer of beards. You intended to make a fool of me, but if I find you here on my return, by God, I will treat you as I am going to treat this Pantafilando!

(Don Quixote goes into the hostel, sword in hand.)

Basile (to Carrasco)
Come! It's all over. (to Maritorne) You really needed to tear my beard off!

Maritorne
My goodness. It was my cow's tail.

Sancho (to Basile, like he's mad)
You! Queen Micomicona! Get out!

Basile
Oh, go to hell.

Ortiz (stopping Sancho)
Pardon! Pardon. But the knight's bill. Who will pay me if they are gone?

Sancho
The bill, what bill?

Ortiz
For staying the night.

Sancho
Pay you, you son of a black woman, for staying the night in hay that should be eaten?

Ortiz
You don't wish to pay me for the night you spent here?

Sancho
It's really you, Algerian! There will never be enough money for me to pay you for such a night.

Ortiz
And my broken jugs, and the figs and the supper?

Sancho
What supper, renegade? (furious) I took nothing from your hovel, on the contrary—

(Sancho goes into the hostel.)

Ortiz
Ah, so that's the way it is!

Carrasco (stopping him)
Come on, be quiet. Here's their bill, with ours!

Ortiz
About time.

Basile (low to Carrasco)
I will take Rosanante and you take the donkey and we will still have them.

Carrasco
That's right.

Basile
Quick, follow me!

(Basile and Carrasco go out by the right.)

Ortiz
Come on, children, since we are awake—

Juanita
Listen

Ortiz
What?

Juanita
That noise.

(The door at the back is opened violently. Two masked men appear;

then Lucinda is dragged in by Don Fernando and Don Antonio. She is masked. All those who surround her are masked.)

Piquilla
Ah, look!

Ortiz (seeing Lucinda)
The lady from before.

Don Fernando
Silence! If one of you knows the name of this lady, let him not pronounce it before the man who is following us.

(Profound silence. Cardenio appears in the doorway, sword in hand.)

Cardenio (blocking the door)
For honest men, gentlemen, you are prompt to flee. But happily, my horse if faster than yours.

Don Antonio
There's nothing between us and you, young man. Be on your way.

Cardenio
You are mistaken. There is this woman. Her cries attracted me to a party in the forest, where a rogue attempted to carry her off. I pursued the wretch, who took flight on seeing me, and I punished him as he deserved. But on my return, this woman had already vanished, dragged off by you—and I intend to know if my sword has more to do in her defense.

Don Antonio
This lady thanks you for your aid. Let that be sufficient for you.

Cardenio
The compliment would be more gracious coming from her own mouth. Let her speak, for she looks much like a certain lady I am following, and I won't let you pass this door until I see her face.

Don Fernando (hand on his sword)
By hell—

Don Antonio (containing him)
Stop, brother. Rage gains nothing. (to Cardenio) You will be satis-

fied, young man, if the lady assures you herself that she is not the one you are seeking?

Cardenio
I am listening!

Don Antonio (to Lucinda)
You understand, Señora, and you know what you must do.

(Lucinda makes an effort to speak, but she cannot.)

Cardenio
Ah, you see quite well—

Don Antonio (stopping him)
The Señora is upset by what has happened. But she will overcome this weakness to reply as she must—(meaningfully) between her brother and her husband.

Cardenio (to Lucinda)
This gentleman is your brother, Señora? And this your husband? And you follow them of your own free will?

(Lucinda makes a sign of assent.)

Cardenio
So—so—you are not Doña Lucinda? (silence, Lucinda gestures negatively) It's your voice I want to hear.

Lucinda (in a choked voice, after a threatening look from her brother)
No!

Cardenio
No! Still—

Don Antonio (stopping him)
Oh, our complaisance is at an end, Señor Cavalier. Now that you are convinced, make way for us so we can continue on our way.

(Cardenio stands aside without taking his eyes off Lucinda.)

Cardenio
It isn't her?

Don Antonio (pulling Lucinda)
Come on, sis.

Don Fernando
Open the door.

(Don Quixote enters from the hostel, sword in hand.)

Don Quixote
Don't open.

Don Fernando (furious)
Again!

Don Quixote
For by El Cid, I will not allow this cowardly magician to escape me disguised as a woman.

(Don Quixote tears off Lucinda's mask.)

Cardenio
Lucinda! To me, my friends.

Don Fernando (to his friends)
To us!

Juanita
Get your knives, boys.

Toreadors
Knives out!

(All three groups make ready to fight.)

Don Quixote (in a thunderous voice)
Toboso! Toboso!

(Suddenly there are three thunderous knocks at the door. Everyone stops.)

Ortiz
Justice!

Corregidor (outside)
Open in the name of the King.

Ortiz
The Corregidor!

(All swords are sheathed. Maritorne opens the door. The Corregidor appears, followed by archers. Day has come. The Corregidor enters gravely and looks everyone over silently.)

Corregidor
Here's a fine woman. What's happening here, Señor Innkeeper?

Ortiz
Oh, milord, don't ask. I think all the devils came here for a rendezvous.

Don Quixote
Not all the devils, but all the Enchanters of La Mancha.

Don Fernando (still masked)
Señor Corregidor, I demand that you do with your authority what our swords were going to do by force. Here's my wife. Order this idiot to give her to me.

Cardenio
Whoever you may be, cowardly thief of love who keeps your face hidden from me—you'll only have her with my life.

Corregidor
Silence, young man! (to Lucinda) Is it true, Señora, that you are the wife of this gentleman?

Lucinda
Alas, too true, to my misfortune.

Corregidor (to Cardenio)
By what right, then, do you keep the lady?

Cardenio
By right of my love for her and her love for me! What they didn't tell you, Señor Corregidor, is that he has obtained the hand of this lady by the blackest treason—and he's fully conscious of his infamy, the coward—since he does not show his face.

Don Quixote
Well spoken, my son!

Corregidor
This young man is right. One doesn't reply to the Corregidor with a masked face. In the name of the King, gentlemen, unmask.

(All unmask except Don Fernando, who hesitates.)

Cardenio
You didn't hear? Unmask!

(Cardenio makes a move to tear the mask off, but Don Fernando prevents him and uncovers himself.)

Cardenio
Fernando!

Corregidor
You, Duke!

Don Fernando
Why not?

Cardenio
Ah, wretch—you! It's you! Ah, you will die by my hand.

(Cardenio lunges at Fernando, but Don Quixote stops him.)

Don Quixote
Peace, my son. One does not assassinate, one fights.

Don Fernando (hand on his sword)
Do your duty, Corregidor, and let's be done with this.

Corregidor (gravely)
You are right, Lord Duke. I will do my duty. You say this woman is

your legitimate wife?

Don Fernando
I have said it, and I repeat it.

Corregidor
Then some here have the effrontery to mock justice.

Don Quixote
Oh, if it were merely justice—but chivalry!

Don Fernando
And what then, Señor Corregidor? Is someone here mocking justice?

Corregidor
You or someone else. Archers, bring in that woman disguised as a man that you arrested on the way.

Don Fernando
But, explain!

Corregidor
Step outside, Lord Duke, and don't interfere.

Don Fernando
But—

Corregidor
I order you outside.

(The duke obeys. Dorothea comes in, between two archers.)

Don Fernando (aside)
Dorothea!

Corregidor
Come forward, Señora. What you told my archers before, when you were arrested—are you prepared to repeat it aloud here?

Dorothea (not seeing Don Fernando)
Since your lordship obliges me, it must be done.

Corregidor
Speak openly, Señora. What did you tell them?

Dorothea
That I was going to rejoin the Duke Fernando, my husband.

All
Her husband!

Don Fernando (aside, stupefied)
Me?

Don Quixote
That villain!

Corregidor (stopping her)
Take care what you say, Señora. Don Fernando doesn't believe himself to be your spouse, because he has already married another woman.

Dorothea
Another wife than me! And who then? Who dares say that?

Don Fernando (coming from behind the Corregidor)
Me! I say it!

Dorothea
Fernando!

Don Fernando (pointing to Lucinda)
I attest that this is my legitimate spouse. And that she who claims the name has no right to it!

Dorothea
She! His wife! Ah, Fernando, recognize me. Look at me. You haven't recognized me. I am Dorothea, it's me. And you cannot have forgotten so much love.

Don Fernando (pushing her away)
I recognize you, Señora, as someone who has never been my wife—but since you force me to say it, you were something worse!

Dorothea
Oh—that word—you won't say it. Señor Corregidor, this man gave me his oath at the foot of the altar. I swear it on the sacred name of God who hears me. And I have proof—I have it. I have it on me.

Corregidor
Wait, Señora. Don't go too far, while there is still time. For if you lie, you'll go to prison forever.

Dorothea (looking for her letter)
Oh, what does that matter to me?

Corregidor
And, if you are telling the truth, he goes to his death.

Dorothea (struck, stopping)
His death!

Don Quixote
That's too little for such a felony.

Corregidor (to archers)
Watch this man! And now, Señora, your proofs!

Dorothea (to herself)
Death! Death! Yes, two wives, it's true.

Corregidor
Come, the proof.

Dorothea (looking at Fernando)
Fernando! This proof, I have—I—I don't have it any more. (resolutely) I haven't got it.

Corregidor
Then you lied!

Dorothea
I lied, yes. I am not his wife. I lied. I lied.

(She collapses in the arms of Piquilla and Juanita.)

Corregidor (giving Lucinda to Fernando)
Lord Duke, here is your wife. Go, you are free.

Cardenio (held by those who surround him)
Never while I am living.

Corregidor (to archers as Antonio, Fernando and Lucinda leave)
Detain this wild man who ignores justice.

Don Quixote
Good! Good! It's only justice but he ignores chivalry which forbids stealing the wife of another.

Cardenio (falling in his arms in despair)
His wife! It's true then!

(They surround Cardenio.)

CURTAIN

ACT III

Scene 7

A savage place in the Sierra Moreno. Large trees cover the entire stage. Mist. In the rear, a grotto, the entry to which is covered with brush. To the right, a large oak.

(A troupe of actors are lying on the grass around a kettle suspended on three sticks. They are finishing their meal. Against the tree is a banner reading "Comedy: Troupe of Angelo the Bad." The devil serves the soup. The Queen gives cutlets to the King and Love passes the cheese.")

Chorus
Across hill and dale,
Strolling players we,
Etc.

Devil
Dining when we can,
Where we can.

Sanchica (passing a plate full of cheese)
Cutting the cheese—

Gracioso
Put it with the fruits.

Princess
Tell me, kiddies, is Sanchica going to go to places where we can find some wine?

Sanchica
By the sun over there—

King (frowning)
They are permitted to be reasonable.

Sanchica
I didn't join you for that. You promised me a crown and pretty clothes. And now you make me do all your dirty work.

All
If you like.

Sanchica (sings)
Oh, if I had realized—
Mommy always told me
Not to play with strangers.
Had I only listened.

King
I will condemn Love to bread and water.

Sanchica
That's it. To bread and water. This is what you call being a Queen. I call it being less than I was before. (sings)

When I was a dairy maid,
I was so happy and free.

Devil
Here's a dollar, little nightingale, and do me the pleasure, without arguing, of getting us some wine.

Sanchica
But—!

King (threateningly)
And if you don't return, we will find you and kill you.

Sanchica (weeping)
Once I led the animals, and now the animals boss me.

(Exit Sanchica.)

King
While we're waiting, let's have a nap.

(They stretch out to nap.)

Basile (separating the branches in the center)
This way. Here's some people. (to comedians) God be with you, comrades. (They look at him without saying a word) You are strolling players I take it?

King
Señor, you see before you players in the illustrious company of Angelo the Bad. (sneezes) Goodnight.

(The comedians return to their naps.)

Basile
Very good. And have you other costumes, coats of armor, etc.?

King
Our trunks are full of them. They're under Gracioso's protection. (points to the clown)

Basile (to Carrasco)
This will do our business. (to Gracioso) Follow me, friend.

Carrasco
Quick! Quick, here they come.

Basile (to Gracioso)
Come, come.

(Basile, Gracioso, and Carrasco vanish to the right behind trees. Enter Don Quixote and Sancho on foot. Don Quixote carries his lance. Sancho carries the saddle bag and the donkey's saddle. The comedians pay no attention and continue their naps.)

Sancho (staggering under the weight)
Ouf!

Don Quixote
Courage, friend, Sancho! Here's the camp of Montesinos where the wise enchanter Tripotin dwells, my sponsor. Here he will tell us how

to rejoin poor Cardenio and show us the divine Dulcinea du Toboso, whom you have never seen—or me, for that matter.

Sancho
Let us see only my poor donkey that was stolen, and I will dispense with the rest.

(Sancho notices the smell of food and sees the kettle.)

Don Quixote (looking at the comedians)
See the prestige of this wise magician. Illustrious Emperors and lovely Princesses don't hesitate to take a siesta before his very door.

(Sancho gets down on his hands and knees and goes to savor the perfume of the kettle and to take a peek inside.)

Devil (his head near the kettle)
Too late!

Sancho
Too late!

(Sancho replaces the cover on the kettle and falls down, overwhelmed.)

Don Quixote (leaning over the King respectively)
Your Majesty wouldn't be able to tell me how I should inform the wise Tripotin of my arrival?

King (half asleep)
Tripotin! We don't have one in our troupe.

Don Quixote (to the Princess)
Lovely Princess, can you tell me?

Princess
When you have stopped boring me.

Don Quixote (aside)
Her heart is spoiled. But perhaps this one here. (to devil) Hey, friend. (nudges him) Friend!

Devil (jumping up, furious and revealing his horns)
By God, why won't you let us sleep peacefully? (goes back to sleep)

Don Quixote (after a moment of silence)
Everything is explained. This forest is enchanted and these people, friend Sancho, are likewise enchanted. This bizarre drowsiness. Right, Sancho? (Sancho replies with a frightful snore) Him, too. And myself, this lassitude. (sits down) The desire to sleep (stretches out) is growing on me. O Tripotin, I abandon myself to your sage will. (snores all around) Teach me through a dream how I can penetrate this enchanted palace and see Dulcinea du Toboso. (sleeping) du Tobo-boso- bo-so!

(Don Quixote has leaned his lance against the trunk of the oak, he now turns his back to the public and sleeps soundly. Gracioso, while still asleep, kicks the kettle which overturns and awakens Sancho.)

Sancho (jumping up, shrieking)
Toboso! Tremble felons!

(Sancho goes to Don Quixote's feet, sits down, and falls asleep again.)

CURTAIN

ACT III

Scene 8

The Dream of Don Quixote

Don Quixote enters bareheaded, and walks about as if someone were speaking to him. He indicates by gestures that a thousand obstacles must be overcome to get to Dulcinea. He goes to the grotto. When he gets there, he is opposed by an army of cactus plants that tickle and scratch him. Battle against the plants, which he wins after an exciting combat. He goes again to enter the grotto. The brush thickens and the flowers turn to the eyes of of owls threatening him. Pine trees bristle with horns and formidable teeth. He separates the brush which disappears this time. There is a large web which covers the opening to the cavern. Seeing a beast, Don Quixote recoils, frightened. The beast climbs to the top of its web and disappears. Don Quixote comes forward to tear off the web. The web is suspended only by a thread. Don Quixote makes an effort to detach it. He battles the web which ends unseen offstage. Finally Don Quixote cuts the web with a blow of his sword and the grotto opens and enlarges. It transforms itself into a fantastic opening in which appears a marvelous palace constructed of stones. Dulcinea is surrounded by her women, who wave laurels at the sight of Don Quixote.

A Voice
Yes, it is she
Who calls you,
Faithful heart.
You see her
Before you.

It's the lady
Of your soul
Who proclaims her
Love to you.
Receive the crown
Which her hand gives
As the reward of your faith.
Sing of Dulcinea.

(During this song, Tripotin signals Don Quixote to come forward. Dulcinea rises and places the crown on Don Quixote's head. Tripotin unites their hands in a magical marriage ceremony.

(The grotto closes and everything disappears. Sound of a Trumpet.

Enter Basile as a squire. His nose is enormous. Disguised thus, he holds a banner. Gracioso blows a trumpet. Basile knocks over the sticks as he traverses the stage in great strides.)

Basile (in a thunderous voice)
Oyez! Oyez! Oyez! All, up and about. Señor Don Quixote, up and about!

(All the comedians leap up, shocked. Sancho, frightened, sits up. Basile goes behind a tree.)

Don Quixote (grabs his lance and jumps up)
Who calls me?

Basile (from behind the tree)
I, the Squire of the Knight of the Mirror, who summons you to advise you that the Lady Cassildee de Vandalie (known as the lady with beautiful red eyes) is infinitely superior in beauty to the very ugly, very stupid, and very impertinent Dulcinea du Toboso, who has only imitation roses, false teeth and wears a wig.

Don Quixote (leaping)
By death!

Basile (nobly)
We will prove it!

Don Quixote (furious)
Where is the bold one who dares say the hair of my Dulcinea is a wig and her teeth false?

Basile
The bold one is here.

(Carrasco appears, armed head to foot and covered with little mirrors.)

Don Quixote (containing his rage and dazzled by the mirrors)
Milord, Knight of the Crazy Head, on what conditions do you please that we square off against each other?

(Carrasco comes closer and gestures that Basile speaks for him.)

Basile
The vanquished must engage from now on to rest his sword and forever renounce chivalry.

Don Quixote
I accept.

(A noble gesture from Carrasco.)

Basile
Sound trumpets! Beat drums.

(Trumpets and drums.)

Don Quixote
My buckler, Sancho, and my helmet.

Sancho (stretched on the ground, still half asleep)
And tell me that I cannot do more than have a nap. There's the barber's bowl.

(Sancho passes the cheese and Don Quixote places it on his head.)

Basile (to Carrasco, low)
Be careful in jousting.

Carrasco
Don't worry. He'll leave without a scratch.

Don Quixote (the cheese starts to fall over his face)
What's this, Sancho? Is my skull softening or my brain melting, or sweat drowning me? But, by The Cid, it doesn't frighten me. Let's go, Knight. Toboso! Toboso!

(The cheese now covers Don Quixote's face. Don Quixote and Carrasco leave, bowing and scraping to each other. All the comedians follow them. Basile stops Sancho who is ready to leave.)

Basile
Halt there, Sir Squire. You know the custom.

Sancho
What custom?

Basile
While the patrons fight with swords, the squires fight with knives.

(Basile pulls out an enormous knife and stands ready.)

Sancho
Sir Squire, that custom lacks common sense. Use your knife to pick your nose if your heart dictates it, but mine is too well made for me to risk ruining it. (starts to leave again)

Basile
If you are revolted by knife fighting, I have another kind of scrimmage to propose to you.

Sancho
But, what an idea, to want us to break our bones for no reason! I've done nothing to you, you've done nothing to me. I like you, you like me. You are handsome. (kisses him, taps his nose) Goodbye. (starts to leave once more)

Basile
Pardon—here are my weapons. (pulls a ham)

Sancho (enthusiastically)
This time I'm with you. (takes the ham) Oh, what a smell. (hugs it to

his heart)

Basile
And what meat! All we need is wine to make it go down.

Sancho (holding the ham)
Good, good! Sit down first. We'll try later to baste it. (sits down to eat)

(Enter Sanchica, running and breathless.)

Sanchica
Here's the wine.

Sancho (stupefied)
Sanchica!

Sanchica (shocked)
Papa!

Sancho
Here! You! My daughter. (jumps up) But, by the devil, what are you doing here, far from your mother?

Sanchica (all aplomb)
They said they would make me Queen, papa.

Sancho
Queen!

Sanchica
Yes! They promised me I'd be a Queen.

Sancho
And you believed that? (to himself) She believed it. Just like her father. (to Sanchica) And you made off without telling your mother? Little rogue.

Sanchica
Oh, I was afraid she would stop me.

Sancho
Like me. And your geese, wretch, and your geese, where are they?

Sanchica
In the country!

Sancho
Alone?

Sanchica
Oh, they don't need people to take care of them.

Sancho (desperate)
I am sure of it. Superb geese. Oh, I had the best with my pigs and my chickens—

Sanchica
Ah, the pig. He escaped.

Sancho
Heavens!

Sanchica
And as for the chickens—Mama killed them all.

(Sanchica makes a sign of wringing their necks.)

Sancho
Murdered!

Sanchica
Yes! Mama said: "What good are the chickens when the hen house is burned?"

Sancho (jumping)
What—the hen house is burned?

Sanchica
Yes, cause my brother left the lamp lit when he ran off.

Sancho
He ran off?

Sanchica
To be a soldier!

Sancho
My son.

Sanchica
He even took all the money you had hidden in the pot.

Sancho (falling in Basile's arms)
Ruined! My chickens, my geese, my children, my money, my donkey! Ruined! Ruined!

Basile (passing the jug of wine to Sancho)
Courage, brother. (Sancho drinks) You still have your wife.

Sancho
Oh, that's what finishes me. She's been left to deal with all this.

Sanchica
You weren't there.

Sancho
She's right. I wasn't there. Yes, you weren't there, stupid donkey. You ran after your kingdom and you didn't think your kingdom was your home, and your government was your household. And everything's gone to the devil—through your fault, imbecile. Well done. And this will teach you, rascal, idiot, stupid beast!

(Sancho beats his chest and tears his hair.)

Basile
Courage, comrade. A rolling stone gathers no moss.

Voices (from outside, shouting)
Victory to the Mirror Knight.

Basile
My master is conqueror.

Sancho
And mine, beaten—as usual.

Basile (removing his nose)
Don't be desolate, friend Sancho.

Sancho
Basile.

Basile
We'll all go back to the old sheepfold.

Sancho
And the donkey, too?

Basile
And the donkey, too.

Sancho (ravished, embracing his daughter)
And the donkey, too!

(Dorothea enters from the right, dressed as a woman, and leading Cardenio.)

Dorothea
This way, Don Cardenio.

Sanchica
My goodness! Our cousin!

Sancho (ready to leave)
And you too, Señora, you will return home. Like us! Like Señor Don Quixote. Wait for us, we will go together. Long live—

(Exit Sancho and his daughter.)

Cardenio
Where have you brought me, Señora?

Dorothea
To your health, perhaps, Cardenio, as well as mine! This way is the one Don Fernando must take and we will wait for him here. I still hope—

Cardenio (interrupting her)
Here he is!

(Enter Don Fernando, Don Antonio and Lucinda.)

Don Fernando (supporting Lucinda)
A moment of rest will restore you, Señora. (seeing Dorothea) Dorothea? You here! (ironically) Still more threats?

Dorothea (softly)
Threats? Oh, no! I don't accuse you, Don Fernando. Here, I forget my pride and who betrayed me. I am suffering, your victim. I fall at your feet.

(Don Quixote appears in the distance and listens.)

Don Fernando
Señora!

Dorothea (on her knees)
Save me! Save these two creatures who love each other and that you have condemned to unhappiness. You turn away, and your hand trembles. You see him. There's nothing here to offend you. And I beg you for a grace that I could claim as a right.

Don Fernando (violently pulling away)
Oh—I expected that word, this right, Señora. This right doesn't exist. And I do not forgive you for invoking it.

Dorothea (rising, softly)
I pardon you. I forgot.

Don Fernando
You pardon me!

Dorothea (softly)
At the foot of an altar, you swore before God that you took me for your legitimate spouse.

Don Fernando
A mere oath. Nothing sacred about it.

Dorothea
Heaven didn't judge it so, since it allowed a priest to hear your words and bless our union.

Don Fernando
If that was true, Señora, you would have some proof of what you

say.

Dorothea
I have such proof.

Don Fernando (laughing)
And having this proof, you did nothing with it?

Dorothea
Perhaps, Don Fernando, because I trembled for you.

Don Fernando
Say rather, because you have nothing more substantial than your lies.

Dorothea
Oh, oh, you are very cruel, too, Don Fernando. If I didn't reveal what chains you to me for life—

Don Fernando
It's because you haven't got it.

Dorothea
I don't have it? Here it is!

Don Fernando (shocked)
This paper?

Dorothea
Decidedly, you have nothing in your soul. You are all witnesses to what I have done to soften this man. I begged. I went down on my knees to him. And you still won't recognize me, Don Fernando? I have too much pride to want you despite yourself. Rather my shame! Of my spousal rights, I have taken only those that will save you. This chain that binds us—here it is! (she throws it at his feet) Burn it! Destroy it! I set you free. And of the past which I efface, nothing remains except the eternal regret I have for having loved for so long such a creature as yourself.

(Exit Dorothea.)

Don Fernando (picking up the paper and looking at it)
This signature. It's true! It's true. This validates the marriage. So

long as this writing remains, Dorothea is my wife. Lucinda is not mine. But it can be destroyed in an instant. She who just left is no more. Well, let it be as Dorothea desires—and this proof destroyed.

(Don Fernando prepares to rip the paper to shreds.)

Lucinda (screaming)
Ah!

Cardenio
Wretch!

(Cardenio seizes Don Fernando's poignard.)

Don Quixote (coming forward)
I heard a supplicant's voice and I saw a woman at the knees of a man, a thing contrary to all laws divine and human. This man would pay dearly if I still had my sword. But today, an oath condemns this arm to slumber. I ask myself if the word of an old man won't have some influence on the soul of a youth too young to be totally corrupted.

Don Fernando (haughtily)
I don't know you—and I don't take advice form anyone.

Cardenio
Listen, then, to prudence, for I have not sworn to keep my sword in its sheath.

Don Quixote
You are wrong, my son, violence calls for violence! But, recall, rather to this man what Doña Dorothea has just done for him and this memory may be worth more than your threats.

(Don Fernando is holding the paper in his hand. He looks at Don Quixote.)

Don Quixote (continuing, heatedly)
Tell him that this betrayed woman, a woman abandoned and humiliated, looked only to his danger. However strong her spousal rights, she preferred to let herself be publicly taken to be his mistress and to save him from his own dishonor.

Don Fernando
It's true. She did that.

Don Quixote (with greater force)
And you see, he hasn't exclaimed with me. O noble, O great and saintly women! You alone are capable of love. Blessed be you, O women, our mothers, our sisters, and our spouses. And cursed be those who scorn you. Cursed be those who outrage you. Cursed be those who blaspheme against you.

All (watching Don Fernando hesitate)
Lord—

Cardenio
Fernando!

Don Fernando (touched)
Cardenio. (to Don Quixote) Thank you. Where is she?

Cardenio
Ah, come.

(Cardenio pulls Don Fernando's arm and they go out together.)

Sancho (comes in, dancing)
Don Quixote's speech. (looks at his master with admiration) Ah, Señor. (falls on his knees before him) What a knight you make when you don't fight.

(Music.)

Don Quixote (looking for his sword)
The clarion!

Sancho (calming him)
No! No! Wedding music. And what a wedding! That of Señor—

Sanchica (running in)
Papa! The wedding! The wedding!

Don Quixote
Then let's take our part in the joys of the world now that all the world is happy.

Sancho
Thanks to you! And let's go home—for as the proverb says—

Don Quixote (frightened)
Sancho!

Sancho
The fool takes longer to cross his house than a wise man to cross a field.

Don Quixote
As for that one, I let it pass. For it is good.

(They all leave.)

CURTAIN

ACT III

Scene 9

A vast green. To the left, the door of a gothic church. To the right, a cabaret. A village feast is going on.

(Don Ortiz, his group, Sancho, Muleteers, Comedians, archers, and peasants are all drinking and eating on benches.)

Chorus
Come, come, let's drink.
The door's open for us.
Drink to the married couple.
Drink and eat forever.

Sancho (ham in hand)
Friends, let's swear in wine
No more kingdoms.
For just to eat
Is enough for me.

Chorus
Drink and eat
Forever.

Children (coming in ahead of the cortège)
Long live the married couple!
Long live the bride and groom!

(People get up to have a look.)

Juanita (on Guerrero's arm)
Oh, my Guerrero, when will you take me to church?

Guerrero
When Núñez takes Piquilla.

Piquilla (to Núñez)
And, when are we going?

Núñez
Same day they do.

All
Long live the newlyweds.

(Music, drums, fifes. The cortège with Gamache and Quitterie enter. Basile leans on Carrasco's arm, who consoles him.)

All
Long live Gamache!
Long live Quitterie!

(At this moment the church door opens and Dorothea comes out. Silence. Only the sound of the church clock is heard. Don Quixote, Lucinda, Cardenio, and Don Antonio appear at the left. At the same moment, Dorothea hesitates and steps back. The group separates to allow her to return. Don Fernando appears.)

Don Fernando
Where are you going, Duchess? The church is waiting for you, and here's your husband to escort you. (bending to one knee)

Dorothea
Ah, Fernando.

(Don Fernando takes her hand.)

All (waving hats)
Long live the newlyweds!

Cardenio
Ah, Lucinda. (hugging her)

All
Long live Cardenio!
Long live Doña Lucinda!

Quitterie
Well, if everyone is marrying the one they love, then, I am going to marry Basile.

Basile
Oh! I'm going to faint. (he does)

All
Love live Quitterie!

Gamache (protesting)
What? What? She's marrying Basile? And I, I who paid for the meal?

Don Quixote (gravely)
You shall pay for the guitars.

Basile (radiant)
You shall pay for the guitars!

(Gamache is dragged off.)

Ballet

(At the end of the ballet, Don Quixote appears on Rosanante and Sancho on his donkey. They are surrounded. The people raise their hats, shouting: "Glory to Don Quixote!" while the dancers continue to twirl around them.)

All
Glory to Quixote!

CURTAIN

ABOUT FRANK J. MORLOCK

FRANK J. MORLOCK has written and translated many plays since retiring from the legal profession in 1992. His translations have also appeared on Project Gutenberg, the Alexandre Dumas Père web page, Literature in the Age of Napoléon, Infinite Artistries.com, and Munsey's (formerly Blackmask). In 2006 he received an award from the North American Jules Verne Society for his translations of Verne's plays. He lives and works in México.

www.ingramcontent.com/pod-product-compliance
Lightning Source LLC
LaVergne TN
LVHW041622070426
835507LV00008B/408